THE
EDUCATION
OF EVERYCHILD

Revised Edition

Ronald Arthur Landor

UNIVERSITY
PRESS OF
AMERICA

Lanham • New York • London

Copyright © 1991 by Ronald Arthur Landor

University Press of America®, Inc.

4720 Boston Way
Lanham, Maryland 20706

3 Henrietta Street
London WC2E 8LU England

Library of Congress Cataloging-in-Publication Data

Landor, Ronald Arthur.
The education of everychild / Ronald Arthur
Landor. — Rev. ed.
p.   cm.
Includes bibliographical references.
1. Education, Humanistic.   2. Education,
Elementary—Philosophy.   I. Title.
LC1011.L33   1991
370.11'2—dc20   91-26341 CIP

ISBN 0-8191-8246-X (paperback, alk. paper)

*To my sons, Barth and Blake; and
to my daughters, Amiel, Regina,
Talitha, and Raissa — a liberal
education in themselves.*

AUTHOR'S ACKNOWLEDGEMENTS

THIS is to express my thanks to the Great Books Foundation, Chicago, IL, for permission to use the Junior Great Books list in Appendix B.

I owe a special debt of gratitude to my wife Miriam for her invariably helpful criticism of this book.

TABLE OF CONTENTS

When one considers in its length and in its breadth the importance of this question of the education of a nation's young, the broken lives, the defeated hopes, the national failures, which result from the frivolous inertia with which it is treated, it is difficult to restrain within oneself a savage rage.

Alfred North Whitehead,
The Aims of Education (1929)

If an unfriendly foreign power had attempted to impose on America the mediocre educational performance that exists today, we might well have viewed it as an act of war. As it stands, we have allowed this to happen to ourselves.

National Commission on Excellence in Education, *A Nation at Risk: the Imperative for Educational Reform*; Gardner, D.P., Chairman (1983), Washington, D.C.: U.S. Department of Education

Chapter I
THE NATURE OF THE PROBLEM

> The greatest and most difficult problem
> to which man can devote himself is the
> problem of education.
>
> Immanuel Kant

T his is a book on education written by an uneducated man; a book on teaching by one who has never been a member of a teaching faculty; a book on the rational foundations of education by one who can claim to have acquired only a few of its appropriate disciplines.

This is not said out of modesty, mock modesty, for notoriety's sake, or to be interesting. Education is composed of rational, objective, and demonstrable elements. The particular attributes of learning that this book describes as comprising the substance of an elementary liberal education are for the most part not among its author's attributes.

It is, as we all know, entirely possible to graduate from institutions even of higher learning without having first acquired even elementary intellectual competencies.

But who is not weary of the subject of education and of all the talk, big and small, about it? Education ought either to be given a decent burial or in some way made to come alive. One possibility of making it come alive would be to start from the beginning and try to define its first steps.

Elementary education appears to baffle those who seek to discover its appropriate substance. What is a more significant sign of the educational times than that we do not know how to educate our children? Nearly everyone agrees that education is a good thing, but — like love, which also appears to find general favor — few agree on what education is or ought to be.

The main purpose of this book is to present the view that genuine elementary education is, of necessity, liberal education, which is distinguished from special, vocational, or professional training by its relevance to every kind of learning and indeed to every part of life.

Genuine education increases the power of the self by extending its dominion over the appropriate disciplines of language. These disciplines are the main human powers of expression. Each of the four major forms of language — the language of words, the language of number, the language of music, and the language of visual art — express the powers peculiar to its own kind. Traditionally, these powers have been known as the liberal arts and the teaching and learning them a liberal education.

The language of words is of course primary. In this language, reading and writing, speaking and listening, are the appropriate disciplines. To teach a child the fundamentals of this primary language is to provide him with the cornerstone of education.

To be able to read a text as written; to be able to write the words that accurately describe, analyze or define a thing, idea, relation, or emotion; to be able to speak effectively and to listen with patience, courtesy, and understanding — these are accomplishments that may take a lifetime to achieve, but childhood is the right time to begin.

The integrity of language is intimately bound up with the integrity of the self; it is not a matter of mere pedantry. We do not ask, "What difference does it make?" in regard to the better or worse exercise of manual or professional skills. Why should we be indifferent to the use of that which most clearly distinguishes a human being from all other creatures?

The liberal arts are the means by which language is used at its best. They are the means by which the languages of learning most notably generate and extend the power of communication.

There are no "non-academic types" who are disqualified by birth, ethnic background, or socio-economic status from acquiring the fundamentals of a liberal education. The liberal arts are democratic in nature. The possibility of learning them is open to all.

"Everyone is elementally endowed with the basic powers of the arts, with that of drawing, for instance, or of music; these powers have to be developed, and the education...built up on them as on the natural activity of the self." (Martin Buber)

It has not been proved that we can't educate every child. What has been proved is that, by means presently employed, we cannot educate any child.

Everychild can be taught to read and to write — and to do these reasonably well; he can be taught to compute and to acquire an elementary understanding of mathematical language and ideas; he can be taught the fundamentals of music and of visual art. He can, in brief, be given an elementary liberal education. The real question is, Are the schools competent to give it to him?*

---

* Whenever the term "Everychild" is used in this book, it is of course meant to apply to both boys and girls. In referring to this term, the masculine pronoun is used only as a matter of custom and convenience.

The appropriate place for beginning a child's liberal education is the First Grade. Because this is not now the practice, liberal education at any grade or at any level has become a relatively rare species, found mostly, it is thought, at certain upper regions of Academe and in constant danger of extinction.

There cannot and will not be much genuine education to be found anywhere at any academic height until it first prevails in elementary education, from the beginning.

A genuine elementary eduction would be one that motivates, nurtures, and inspires the student's own serious investment of intelligence and imagination.

Not all students in a program of this kind would derive the same benefits from it. But it would be sufficiently varied in scope to meet the educational needs of both the gifted and the less gifted of all the students enrolled.

The widely differing aptitudes called for in each of the four languages of learning (and their complementary disciplines) correspond generally to the diffuse distribution of the gift for learning inherent in all children by virtue of their faculties of imagination and intelligence.

These faculties are not only distributed in different degrees but according to different kinds of aptitude. The child who is weak in science and mathematics may very well possess an aptitude for music, visual art, or poetry.

The program in mathematics, for example, would be sufficiently elementary for major ideas to be grasped by those with little mathematical talent, and yet sufficiently deep — as the truly elementary is — to motivate the interest of even the mathematically inclined student.

Other fields of study call forth similarly varied configurations of talent.

Intellectual and imaginative gifts are not only distributed variously but are exercised with varying degrees of initiative and economy — which fact may in the long run and in the end result be more significant than the initial pattern of distribution.

If the curriculum is appropriately proportional and reasonably devised, it will provide the nourishment and nurturing that will adequately meet the educational needs of all its participants, however unequal their endowments, providing only that these fall within at least the ordinary range of intelligence.

The gifts of learning may be distributed unequally, but the need of children to cultivate those gifts that they have is equal in all. Who is to say how the nurturing of lesser talent in one child may not have more beneficial influence upon his life and that of his society than the cultivation of greater talent in another? Or who is to say that it is less important to encourage and nurture those gifts in children who are starved for cultivation that those who are not?

But, fortunately, there is no necessity to decide whether or not we are going to provide a bonafide elementary education for one child rather than for another; nor is there necessity to decide whether or not we are going to meet one genuine educational need rather than another. The best kind of elementary curriculum would educate all participants, and no legitimate educational need would be denied or lack opportunity for nurture.

Elementary education requires a definition and design that it does not now have. Because the schools do not make educational sense, educational chaos rages there — not to mention other varieties of disorder.

The educational model described in this book makes allowance for no significant exceptions. It is intended simply to define elementary education in terms of its fundamental principles. Lacking such definition, there can neither be a rational order — that is, a real educational system — nor the exceptions that experience reveals to be necessary or wise.

This book is much less concerned with criticizing our schools than in establishing, if possible, their proper educational responsibilities. No well-informed person in our society need any longer be told that, by and large, our school system is failing and has been failing for a long time. It is pointless to beat a dead horse and heartless to beat a sick one.

The justification for criticism of what the schools are failing to do is to clear the ground for a constructive description and definition of what they ought to do.

There is little evidence that the schools have improved since the Olden Days when the author attended them and boyhood was in flower. The day before yesterday education was Progressive. Yesterday education was New — New Math, New Science, New History. Today: What?

Not knowing our educational destination, we hope to discover it by taking various routes — simultaneously. If everything is tried at least once, something — especially if it be new or Electronic — is bound to succeed. Although it is well established in the democratic ethos that all children ought to receive an elementary education, it is not clear what this means.

It was once assumed that anyone who knew the three Rs had had an adequate elementary education. But aside from these — which provide, whether in Traditional, Progressive, or New modes of styling, skimpy covering at best — there was and is no strictly defined understanding of what constitutes adequacy in this regard. The problem is ancient:

> That education should be regulated by law... is not to be denied, but what should be the character of this public education, and how young persons should be educated, are questions that remain to be considered. As things are, there is disagreement about the subject. For mankind are by no means agreed about the things to be taught, whether we look for virtue or the best life. Neither is it clear whether education is more concerned with intellectual or with moral virtue. The existing practice is perplexing; no one knows on what principle we should proceed — should the useful in

life, or should virtue, or should the higher knowledge, be the aim of our training; all three opinions have been entertained. (Aristotle, *The Politics*)

Deciding "on what principle we should proceed" is even more perplexing now than in any previous time in history, not least because now we are concerned with the education of all children and not simply those of a privileged class.

But unless we become clearer than we are about the principle by which we should proceed, we won't stand much chance of getting anywhere worth being, no matter how many billions we spend in transit. If formal, institutional education should be seen and evaluated as a unity so that the several areas of study within elementary school, high school, college, graduate school, as well as between these different levels, relate in a cohesive way to each other according to a comprehensive principle — what principle could be said to hold our system together? What gives it educational unity? What is its consistent philosophy? In fact, how or in what way can it reasonably be called an educational *system*?

If we don't begin with a sound idea of education, how can we hope to conclude with a sound educational system? If we don't first effectively state the problem, how can we hope to solve it? If we don't know the results that we want and ought to want, how can we establish our priorities?

Moreover, we are not likely to become clearer in our understanding of how we should proceed in the education of children unless there is a radical improvement in the discussion about it. This book purports to be no more than a step in that direction. Undoubtedly, it too often expresses the obvious or neglects the essential. In the midst of chaos, it is not always possible to know what can be taken for granted.

But although major educational questions are raised in this work, it is not thought that all the answers to them are proposed here.

One answer, however, is: namely, that the teaching and learning of language in its several major forms — literary, mathematical, musical, visual — and as exemplified by individual works of art in which these forms are powerfully, memorably, and characteristically expressed and discussed is the main principle on which education should proceed.

There are, needless to say, many particulars of the program here proposed that require more detailed consideration than is here given them. Presumably, this will not present insuperable difficulties where there is agreement in principle.

The intelligence, imagination and initiative of an educational enterprise is evidenced not only in essential and fundamental ways, but also in the interstices of the program — the style, utility, wit, elegance, of the incidental learning with which the Grand Tour is conducted. There is a great deal of incidental intelligence — and some of it not so incidental — that a good educational system will transmit to its students.

Every educational system educates its own kind of teacher. The kind of system recommended in this book requires that liberal artists in each of the languages of learning teach the arts that belong to these languages. The typical "education" course in schools or departments of education should be considered *verboten*, as not belonging to Education but to School, a wholly different proposition.

That "good teachers are born, not made" may be true of geniuses of the profession, the rare few; but teaching is a craft as well as an art. The techniques of good discussion should be considered essential to education, transmittable by persons who are somewhat less than geniuses to others similarly endowed.

Discussion is not the only valuable teaching method, but it is the central one in liberal education. There are all too few good discussion leaders, born or made; but there would be many more if it were generally understood that leading a discussion is a technique as well as an art and, like any other technique, its principles and practices can be analyzed, studied, and transmitted.

The ability to ask good questions is the hallmark of a good discussion leader. But what is a good question? This question itself goes to the heart of the learning process. It is interesting — and depressing — that our educational institutions appear so little taken up with it. "What is a question?" asks Eva Brann, Dean of St. John's College, Annapolis, Maryland. "To ask about asking is the most reflexive of all reflective questions and therefore the most crucial."

The inability or unwillingness to raise the question of questioning in a serious way is the other side of School's assumption that it knows what it is doing. To those who have no doubt that they are right, the question mark can only seem a threatening sign.

In a class discussion of a text the opening question, if logically and imaginatively followed, should lead to at least a tentative resolution.

The object of the discussion should not be seen as simply a gathering of different opinions on the issue. Participants should be challenged to defend their opinions. If a better — i.e., a truer—understanding of the question under discussion is not its primary purpose (along of course with sharpening the skills of reading, speaking, listening, essential to the thinking that leads to better writing)— what is?

A good discussion stimulates interest, excitement, even passion if the issue is significant enough, so that it will engage the fullest attention of the student and be felt to matter whether or not there is a pertinent and fruitful development of the issues in question, and not merely turn into an "intellectual" gabfest.

Good discussion not only helps develop valuable human skills, but also emphasizes and cultivates the understanding that ideas frequently have practical consequences.

If questioning is a major form and spirit of a liberal education, skill in performance is its substance. It is the premise of this book, that Everychild is capable of learning to perform the liberal arts, appropriate to each of the languages of learning, with competence at least and with excellence at best, according to age, native endowments, and willingness to learn.

The real education of teachers ought to be considered as taking place primarily in their own educational institutions. Teachers in the same school or college should be in continual discussion with each other about how best to communicate ideas and issues that bear upon every part of the program.

The assumption is fair that every teacher in the school, no matter how many years of experience, he may have had — which may simply mean the repetition of teaching poorly — is there to learn as well as to teach. And how else should the teachers of a school learn from each other unless they have first-hand knowledge by observation of the teaching actually being done in each other's classrooms? Good teaching becomes even more rare than it is when it lacks the benefit of the informed criticism that every art requires.

What is of much greater importance than the effort to anticipate and resolve all the details that would have to be considered in carrying out the program described in this book is the firm conviction that an elementary liberal education for all children, along the lines suggested herein, is feasible and worthwhile; and that it might prevail anywhere that School now does.

If this program would appear to the teacher of a typical fifth or sixth grade class as unrealistic — she (or he) may be right. By the time a child has spent five or six years in the typical School system, he has, predictably, developed into a typical School student.

Furthermore, there is so much waste, incompetence, and disorder in the present School management of the student's learning, that it would be difficult for anyone to have confidence in a program administered by the schools and based on the assumption of ten, productive, intellectually significant years.

The ultimate criterion of an educational institution is that it use its students well.

Specifically, this means that an elementary or secondary school (or liberal arts college) may best evaluate its success in achieving appropriate educational objectives by how well it cultivates the skills, intelligence, and imagination of its students.

Here is where (1) materials of learning (good books); (2) teaching methods (primarily discussion that engages the minds of students more usefully than being temporary receptacles for use in passing tests); and (3) teaching ability (the teacher as an artist — or at least a good craftsman — and a model of how to learn), become essential.

These are not utopian considerations but bedrock factors in providing the beginnings of a genuine education for Everychild.

However novel this program may at first appear, it should be emphasized that the most important parts of it can hardly be regarded as original or even experimental.

The primacy of language in the education of a child (and the understanding of "language" as the language of words, of mathematics, of music, and of visual art); the use of discussion as a principal teaching method; the emphasis upon individual works of art as learning materials; the employment of teaching artists and craftsmen of the several learning disciplines as the appropriate teachers — this is hardly new or untried doctrine.

But what makes it seem revolutionary in present circumstances is the distance that the schools have come from these fundamentals. As a consequence, our society has not only lost confidence in the serious education of children but has even forgotten what this might be.

It cannot be stated too emphatically that lack of money for education is not the problem. The United States spends more money per capita on education than any country in the world.

Lack of competence, lack of efficiency, lack of understanding the principles of how to proceed, are what ail the schools.

The more we believe that lack of money is the problem, the more likely it is that the way to a genuine education for our children will be obscured, denied, ignored.

The Program proposed in this book for children six to sixteen need not cost a dime more than the non-education they are getting now.

Waste, inefficiency, and incompetence, are more expensive in the long run— and not only for education — than doing the job well in the first place. "How much more," writes John Stuart Mill in his Autobiography, "than is commonly supposed may be taught, and well taught, in those early years which, in the common modes of what is called instruction, are little better than wasted."

The question is not whether Everychild is capable of being educated, but whether the schools are ready, able, and willing to educate him. If— and it is a large if — from the beginning, from the First Grade, education were substituted for what is now egregiously recognizable as School, a genuine education for all could be given there.

Beyond this it is a question of public policy; whether or not the people of this nation will demand a decent education for their children.

To be serious in anything is to be honest according to its necessity. To be serious is to be in accord with the truth of the occasion; not to be solemn when the need is comic, not to be a clown if the situation requires responsible words or deeds.

To be serious about the reform of our educational system, we must begin from the beginning, from the First Grade. When we have first resolved the problem of elementary education, we shall then be in a position to do something worthwhile about changing the rest of the educational enterprise, up to and including graduate departments and professional schools.

Higher education can't be looked to as the lever that can or will raise up the schools because, lacking a clear and effective idea of its own nature, it can't even raise itself up. "We could administer this university if only the students would give us back the administration building," was its cry in the Sixties. The superficial, patchwork, curriculum proposals suggested in the last several decades by college and university reformers — who focussed upon the schools but had little to say about college and university reform — indicate that most of them have little or no idea of a kind of elementary or preparatory education radically different from the one we have.

Where there is no principle by which to proceed, distinctions vanish. If the public lacks an effective idea of what education is and what the schools should be doing — an idea that clearly distinguishes School from Education — the use of political action to change the schools will only compound the confusion.

The desperate need to improve education in the schools is nationwide. All the children of America (white, black, red, brown, yellow; rural, urban, suburban, inner city) should have comparable educational opportunities. This will occur only by local, state, and federal governments and private schools working together with a common purpose — which means an agreement in principle upon how education ought to proceed.

The best education is both traditional and revolutionary.

The values and ideas that enable us to understand and live in the present are obviously not the exclusive fruit of here and now. We live in remembrance and anticipation, as well as in immediacy. An older man's look of youthfulness may reflect ideals of his youth that vibrate in him still, a fidelity to certain memories and thoughts of the past to which he stubbornly clings. Time pulls him forward but memory and imagination look back, making vital the span of the present. How can we live in the present as if the past has no meaning for it? or face the future as if the present does not bear upon it?

But there is nothing of the past that a present generation should want to take over in an unexamined kind of way.

Education is revolutionary insofar as it is responsive to the spirit, the reality, the language, of present need. It is revolutionary insofar as the power is engendered to break with stale, worn-out ways of being and thinking and to discover and invent new, more effective ones.

When immediate and pressing needs require new ways of looking at them — that is, "a new birth of freedom" — it is a revolutionary spirit that we want. But fortunate are we to be able to find this spirit in a clear line of descent from one "our fathers" conceived.

When genuine education becomes increasingly available for all, the way will be increasingly open to bring the intelligence of all directly to bear upon problems of the common good. The corollary of "what touches all should be approved by all," is that, "what should be approved by all is capable of being understood by all." Jefferson's vision of a whole people participating directly in the affairs of their own government can be transformed into reality only as we transform School into

Education. No educational system of any nation in history has ever provided the fundamentals of a liberal education for all. Only a democracy could do it and only a democracy would want to do it.

Ten years are not too long a time to acquire an elementary understanding and competent use of the liberal arts, but they are not long enough to learn to live one's life. A liberal education is one that contains within itself the potent means and high incentive of continuing education for a lifetime.

We must begin by taking education seriously: not, primarily, its economics, or its politics, or its sociology, or its technology, but the understanding of its nature; first and foremost, its philosophy, the principle or principles by which it should proceed.

Education naturally tends to become liberal education when it is taken most seriously. When the discussion of important ideas is given precedent over the pursuit of trivia; when the teacher as liberal artist presents a good example of what it means to be a good learner; when individual works of art in all four of the languages of learning are accorded their rightful place as education's most powerful mediators between language and reality — this is liberal education and it is education as its best.

For Everychild nothing else is good enough.*

* For a capsule presentation of the program of elementary liberal education proposed in this book, see Appendix A.

Chapter II
SCHOOL VS. EDUCATION

Education is something which should be apart from the necessities
of earning a living, not a tool therefore. It needs contemplation,
fallow periods, the measured and guided study of the history
of man's reiteration of the most agonizing question of all:
Why? Today the good ones, the ones who want to ask
why, find no one around with any interest in
answering the question, so they drop out,
because theirs is the type of mind which
becomes monstrously bored at the
trade-school concept.

John D. MacDonald

American children are not deprived of the opportunity to go to school. Our problem is what to do with them once they get there. No one would be so bold as to claim that the schools are now solving this problem with distinction.

Children start out in school avid to learn. They come to the first grade full of wonder, of interest, of hope. They are eager to co-operate with whatever is asked of them. But so little of value is asked that in time and inevitably their interest begins to wane. It then becomes a question mainly of their ability to hang on. School is an endurance contest that nobody wins. Students get Bored and teachers get Burn-out.

Childhood is the time to acquire the fundamentals of liberal education. The good books that mean so much when read as a child will never again find so appropriate an occasion. The waste of years in elementary education becomes, perforce, the waste of years at the secondary level also. Not unpredictably, this leads either to the intellectual disillusionment and despair of the school dropout or the student at the college and university level discovering that the great intellectual adventure to which he had looked forward with such anticipation as a deliverance from School — is only School all over again.

Whatever the laws and administrative regulations — policy, party, and power struggles — that would prevent the schools from initiating a serious program of elementary education, there is at any rate no "research" (upon which billions of dollars are spent every year in this country) that would have to be done, there is nothing essential that we do not already know, there are no resources that are not already at hand, to begin and to get on with the job.

The arts of language have existed since the dawn of human culture. They are older than the cave paintings at Altamira and as new as the latest poem or play, painting or scientific idea, music or mathematics, that are worth taking seriously.

Although the smoke of confusion may accompany the flame of revolution, it is also true that where there is smoke, there may be only smoke. A student in the schools of fifty years ago would feel in perfectly familiar surroundings in the schools today, despite yesterday's New Math and today's electronic hoop-la.

We must not take change in jargon for the real changes that are needed to bring about Education where now there is only School. As long as the School mentality controls the situation, School will neither die nor fade away.

School is a world apart. The language of liberal art is not spoken there.

School introduces the student to the real world tritely, superficially, meanly. Much does he travel there in the realms of tin and many claptrap states and kingdoms see. The weakness of School is as the weakness of ten because its mind is confused.

If we had no other way to describe the confounding of intelligence that we call School except in terms of the principle by which it proceeds, what could be said of it except that there is no such education?

The difficulty of grasping the form by which the nature of School can be understood undoubtedly accounts in part for public bewilderment in trying to understand what it is and how it should function. It is not incomprehensible that the public should feel ambivalent about an institution whose essential nature is so anomalous.

School is a hot-bed of Gresham's laws. It is where non-books drive out real books; non-teachers drive out real teachers; Doctors of Education drive out real educators; lectures drive out discussion; facts drive out ideas; tests drive out thinking; driver-training courses drive out language courses. In a word, School drives out Education.

The fetish of grades, the textbook imitation of books, the incompetent teachers, the unintelligible curriculum, the unimaginative leadership, the intellectually wet milieu — all this is School, not Education.

School gives Education a bad name; it is a graveyard of Education. The best evidence that School has zeal but not according to knowledge is School's most potent argument *for* Education; namely, there's money in it; a diploma pays.

The pressure increases as one ascends the ladder. It asks a great deal of a young person — often more than he can bear — to wait out the long, time-wasting, anxiety-inducing, intelligence-insulting school years until such time as he shall come into his economic reward. There must be a better reason than this for education. The price is too high for the prize, and even the putative reward often proves chimerical.

The difference between the best public schools and the worst in this country is considerable, and this difference matters. But compared to the kind of education that might be given Everychild, the one provided him now by the nation's schools is fair at best but at worst unspeakable, the intellectual equivalent of garbage.

There is of course a wide range of difference among private schools also. However, the private schools of the country cannot be said to offer the alternative of a radically superior kind of education. Despite the fact that they are comparatively free to make up their own curriculum, select their own books, and establish their own criteria for the qualifications of their teachers, they do not in general use this freedom in a particularly bold, innovative, imaginative or distinguished kind of way. By and large, they appear satisfied to parallel the public schools, except that they claim to be able to do the same things better.

School and Education are two radically different approaches to learning. The child goes to School under compulsion and there finds himself captive of all he surveys. School is a center for the waste of thought and the abatement of imagination. A non-think holding tank.

Education is everything that School is not; it makes sense in itself, and not merely as economic or social expedience; it is the difference of kind between growing a little or dying a little every day.

All the vast administrative clutter that School accumulates, like a deranged collector who has long since forgotten why he ever wanted the stuff in the first place, is symptomatic of the sickness of educational life in this country, of its intellectual despair and disarray*. School is not generally known for touching the imagination, except to waste it.

But to suppose that School can be transmuted into Education by the mere reduction of administrative personnel is to take the symptom for the cause.

The main problem is not how to get less administration, but how to get more Education. The two aims are not necessarily related as cause and effect. The persistent problem of school administration is that the schools lack a serious, viable, appropriate, educational policy to administer. They lack a commanding principle by which to proceed.

Lacking this knowledge, they are unable to establish convincing and stable priorities, unable to adopt effective teaching methods, unable to devise a rational curriculum, and unable to select the materials of study that will achieve the best educational results.

No realistic assessment of the schools as educational institutions can be made except by means of a coherent, comprehensive, and commanding idea of what education is — and is not. Where there is no such idea, what is there to justify the schools, and how is one to understand their mere existence — except perhaps as a way of keeping the kids off the street?

Because there is no present agreement upon the results for which the schools should be held responsible, there is no consensus upon the results that are being achieved. Each observer evaluates "results" in his own way. Needless to say, School officials tend to be partial to their own results, such as they may be.

*"Ratio of administrators to students in Chicago's public schools: 1:43; in Chicago's parochial schools: 1:6,250." (Harper's "Index", November 1988)

What, indeed are educational results? This is of course but another way of asking, How should children be educated? It doesn't seem unreasonable that there may be a kind of education that is good for every child.

Because educators are generally held to be peculiarly vulnerable to the insinuations of idealism, a warm appreciation for the power of money in educational affairs is taken as evidence of a sound understanding of educational reality. But more money or less administration are not necessarily and invariably relevant to the problem of transforming School institutions into Educational ones.

Money spent on electronic gadgets as the new bright hope for education buys what money can buy — machines — but does not necessarily buy education. The seriousness with which we take the education of Everychild is measurable less by what we are willing to spend on it than by how we are willing and able to think about it.

In the circumstances more education is surely needed, but not more time-serving. Additional years of schooling cannot be taken as tantamount to the advancement of learning. More eduction is needed from the beginning — from the First Grade — but not more School-time tacked on in the hope that this will do what has not been done previously by the same means.

No institution in our society has so fiercely resisted change of any essential kind (even to the extent of developing elaborate means of simulating change) than schools. No institution in our society provides so poor a return for the money invested. No institution in our society meets its responsibilities in a less effective and more mediocre way. And nowhere is the need for the first-rate more evident than in the education of children.

The nature of education must determine the curriculum, not the other way around. Procrustes was a social engineer, not an educator. The nature of education is suggested by the capabilities of a human mind and the quality of the resources available to develop it, both of which are rather more considerable than School credits either to be.

School *versus* Education will be, one could confidently predict, an issue a hundred years from now. But every perennial issue has an immediate one to represent it. It is the immediate issue, the present condition of the schools, which confronts the living generation.

A realistic view compels the recognition that School, in one form or another, will be with us always. But despite this disagreeable fact of life, there is room for hope that the schools can be changed for the better and that Everychild can be given the fundamentals of Education, where now he is only Schooled.

If we had a clear idea of the kind of education that children ought to be getting, we might be able to find the ways of providing it. American genius for the practical side of life, for common sense, for the real and for the possible, have been deeply frustrated in the endeavor to build a first-rate educational system.

An instinct for what is real must lead us toward the substance of education and away from the cheap facsimile thereof. It is Education that is wanted. What could be more impractical than a huge school establishment that fails so dismally to educate? School buildings only take money to build, but the education that should go on inside them takes nothing less than the best thought of mankind. Practicality of one kind gets a school plant built, but the building won't be educationally practical unless eduction is what occurs inside.

American children go to schools that are, for the most part, intellectual slums. Naturally, children are not immune to the intellectual disorders that they encounter there. There is nothing in life more potentially alive than a child's imagination and intelligence. We would not tolerate our children being made into physical cripples. How can we tolerate their being made into mental ones?

School children are taught in ways that stunt their intelligence and deplete their imagination, and this great School robbery goes on every day in most classrooms in the country. Selma Fraiberg, writing of the teaching of English in our schools declares, "There is no part of this curriculum that can be singled out for repair. It all hangs together, from the first grade through the twelfth, a dilapidated structure based upon bad reading, poor instruction, repellent texts, and a degraded literature.... The failure of our present methods of reading and language instruction derives essentially from a failure in understanding the psychology of language."

Professor Fraiberg doesn't blame the children or their parents for this problem. Clearly, it isn't a weakness of the juvenile will or intelligence that accounts for it. The problem is simple: School does not know how to educate. Children are caught squarely in the middle between compulsory education (plus the Indispensable Diploma) on the one hand, and the incompetence of the schools on the other.

Intellectual slums cannot be redeveloped by the use of one makeshift after another. For every New, Exciting, and Challenging gimmick that fails, two spring up in its place, federally or foundation financed.

Discontent with the schools should not prompt nostalgia for some imagined academic glory of the past. As far as genuine liberal education for all is concerned, School never had a Golden Age.

However, it ought not be forgotten or in any way depreciated, that in an earlier period of our history, the "common school" was successful in helping to establish a common culture and in giving millions of immigrants a leg up the ladder of opportunity in the New World. But in this day and age the reservoir of good will that these accomplishments created has run out. The schools have entered a new era. America has become another kind of New World. It is not "acculturation" but education that is required of the schools today.

Not every mind can grow to the same height. But the height that real education can help Everychild attain depends not a little upon the assumption that is made of his potentialities and upon the expectation entertained of his intelligence. It depends upon our paying less attention to his wants and more attention to his needs. It depends less upon what we give him (except in the way of opportunity) than upon what he is motivated to give of himself.

The same philosophy that justifies equal protection of the law for all requires also that all be held equally educable. The liberal arts are no more the peculiar province of the highly intelligent than moral education is of the highly virtuous. Ordinary intelligence is sufficient for all the good purposes of life, including a good education.

As there are not two kinds of justice to be administered by the state; so, too, there are not two kinds of human intelligence to be educated.

Intelligence functions to understand the intelligible and is of the same nature among all children of humankind. That all children are "equally educable" does not of course mean that all are equally intelligent, but that all have the same kind (not degree) of intelligence to be educated.

What this means in effect is that there are no major forms of language — plus the skills that accompany them — that cannot or should not be taught to all children of at least ordinary intelligence. Because all have the same kind of intelligence, all are in need of the same kind of education. In a democratic society, the liberal arts are for all. Children are in general more intelligent for their ages than adults for theirs. (Think of how much an infant learns in his first year of life.) This is not intended as flattery of the juvenile mind, but simply to suggest that intelligence can be cheapened, frustrated, deflected, aborted, dissipated — and that this is in fact what School does.

The mind is insulted and injured not by use, but by disuse or misuse. The mind of the child is mistreated by *not* providing him the means of using it well; by *not* giving his intellectual and imaginative faculties their due; by *not* teaching him the forms of language that are the main instruments of communication; by *not* ensuring that he encounter the works of art and quality of language that he needs for genuine education.

If a child is not "bright," we do not think that there is any mystery as to why he doesn't do well in school. But why do so many obviously intelligent youngsters do so poorly?

It is a nice point as to which fact is more appalling — the frequently high caliber of school dropouts or the dismal intellectual results evident in school graduates. Possibly, these two facts bear some significant relation to each other.

Defenders of the School system declare that the dropout rate has decreased, not increased, since the beginning of the century. This misses the point. Dropouts weren't recognized as a problem until there came to be required a diploma, degree, certificate, or reasonable facsimile thereof, for most employment or advancement in society. As it is — and insofar at least as accurate records are available — one out of every three students drop out today before getting their high school diploma.

If this paper curtain didn't stand between the preferments of life and a young lad's pluck and luck, who would be so careless of years of his life as to want to spend them at educational institutions that do not educate?

Moreover, when "education" means no more than the way a job can be found, it comes in time to mean not even this. To persevere through the school grades and still discover oneself lacking in the intellectual graces is depressing enough, but to have still to remain outside the promised land of regular employment and higher fringe benefits after receiving one's high school diploma is enough to drive one to Higher Learning in spite of himself.

The education of Everychild must be one to which he can respond with the best of his ability. The schools perpetrate a fraud by "protecting" him from excellence on the grounds that he is not ready for it. Not ready in elementary school. Not ready in high school. Never ready. Always the bridesmaid.

School students are regarded as being in a perpetual state of getting ready to get ready. Kindergarten casts a long shadow. School starts at Anywhere, is rarely Somewhere, arrives at Nowhere right on time for Commencement.

In the time that it takes a school student to travel the distance between the place where he is and the place where his education is supposed to be, it has in the meantime moved on.

Because the schools do not know the answer to the fundamental question of how to bring student and education together, the common practice is to shove this question up — to the level above, which in turn does the same.

As a consequence, even college has come to be regarded in recent years as primarily a place of getting ready for graduate study, where the really serious learning is supposed to begin. No wonder the value of the bachelor's degree has gone down. Every Babe A Doctor has a grand democratic ring. King Demos is wearing a doctoral cap and gown these days, even if he is unemployed.

School hovers over childhood as a constant threat. The children are the victims, though they may not know it. Many will never know it. They will assume that that is the way education is. It is not supposed to be any different. It always was this way and it always will be.

School students, for the most part, are not in a position to analyze the peculiarities of the system under which they are victimized. This system is hardly any respecter of color, class, or caste (although children from the worst neighborhoods are usually the worst victims).

The students don't know how to change the system for the better. If it's not changed for them, it won't be changed.

If School and Education could be equated with each other, the responsibility of the child for his performance in school would be more obvious. But despite the notorious unwillingness of school teachers and administrators to take responsibility for the failure of the schools, the American public has found it increasingly difficult to believe that the responsibility for this failure belongs primarily to the children and their parents.

The failure of the schools to educate is more than ironic: it is a moral outrage.

In the past forty or fifty years the freedom of the child has been vastly extended and his status abnormally elevated — along with a corresponding decrease in what has been asked and expected of him. The diminution of responsibility at home was matched by the diminution of academic standards and requirements in school. Parents and teachers appeared to agree that expectations of higher performance would either be cruel and unusual punishment or they would (horrors!) inculcate feelings of "guilt" in him.

The outcome of this general lowering of parental and academic requirements was, quite naturally, a lowering of the child's achievement: an idiotization of childhood. In certain primitive tribes an idiot is regarded as an object of worship. In our society we demean the child as an intelligent and moral being (with all the duties and responsibilities, as well as rights, privileges, and immunities thereunto appertaining) as the price of raising his status and extending his freedom.

Not a primitive but an idiot society is the parody of a civilized one. Pip in the captain's cabin.

The opportunity to attend School is one thing; that of getting a decent elementary education quite another. The School dropout may not be able to describe this difference anymore precisely or elegantly than by saying that School just doesn't add up, and that all he wants is out. And out he goes — with precious little to show for ten or more long tedious years of school.

Moreover, one must further distinguish between those who drop out of School in actual fact and those who might be described as "inward dropouts," giving as little of themselves to the situation as is necessary to get their diplomas. The depth of the wound that School inflicts is not conducive to maximum effort.

School fails — and fails miserably — because, among other things, it doesn't know the results it wants and ought to want.

Consequently, instead of deciding upon appropriately desirable and realistic goals, School typically substitutes inspirational rhetoric — psychological goals or ideals, the achieving of which could hardly be intended in any seriously accountable way.

School systems that declare their objective to be that of giving their students "spontaneity, joy, and self-confidence," or "the courage to adapt them to the challenges of a changing world," or the ability "to face unpleasant tasks with the knowledge that through perseverance they can overcome them," or the magic that would enable "each child to live a happy life," — all gifts devoutly to be wished —

are clearly extending their reach further beyond their grasp than could possibly bear any credible relation to the curriculum.

It would certainly be lovely if education could "help each learner...to develop satisfactory answers to universal questions such as 'Who am I?' 'Where am I going?'" But, given the schools' present ineffectiveness in developing more elementary skills, one would not be well advised to bet on it.

The ineffectiveness of the schools is so monumental, and the distance between its professed goals and its actual achievement is so extensive and so bizarre, that if School didn't exist it would take a comic genius to invent it.

To perform well in a work that engages significant human qualities gladdens the soul; incompetence is depressing. Achievement is an extension of the self and is measurable by objective criteria.

We short-change a youth by not asking of him the best of which he is capable. It's a slob's world that has no elegance, no style, to motivate and inspire him. To ask greatly is to confer dignity. We are so fearful of asking of the child more than we think he can give, that we make the opposite — and worse — mistake of asking much less, thereby diminishing the possibilities of his achievement and diminishing him.

Achievement is a hallmark of growth. Instead of asking much of our children, we dream of how much we can give them. The dream of parents becomes a nightmare of their children.

The elementary education that Everychild should have will not be given him if the nature of childhood is either sentimentally elevated, as where the child is considered competent to shape his own education; or where he is regarded as an inferior type whose education need not be taken as seriously as an adult's.

Recognition of the child as a person whose dignity, honor, intelligence are no different in kind from that of an adult is a necessary pre-condition of an education that is no different in kind. Modern culture freed the child from what it conceived as the unjust authoritarianism of the parents, but failed to provide him with the understanding and competencies that his new freedom required.

The beginning stage of education is at least as important as the later ones, and the child himself will never in his life be more serious about his education than he is the first day in the First Grade. "It will perhaps be wondered, " wrote John Locke, "that I mention *reasoning* with children: and yet I cannot but think that the true way of dealing with them. They understand it as early as they do language; and, if I misobserve not, they love to be treated as rational creatures sooner than is imagined." [italics his]

Unless the schools have respect for the child's seriousness, and take it seriously, and match it with a seriousness of their own, a seriousness that evidences itself in the education of teachers, in the selection of learning materials, in the composition of the curriculum, and, above all, in an atmosphere in which intelligence and imagination are sovereign — unless the schools themselves become as serious as this, the seriousness of their students will and does disappear.

There is no better time for the education of Everychild to turn serious than Grade One, and no better way for it to continue than steady on this course.

Do you see that boy looking out the classroom window, day-dreaming? He doesn't much care what is going on in the room. His experience has been that if he knew, it would be sure to prove depressing. Better to live in a dream world — if he is to be kept from a real one — until he has a chance to discover the real world for himself. He has no way of expertly evaluating what goes on in that classroom. It might be worth something — and then again it might not. But there is all too little evidence to indicate that he should commit himself to the situation as he sees it. (And in this situation whose judgment can he trust other than his own?) If by some unforeseeable chance, School were to become real — that is, really important and not just touted as such — he might respond in kind. He might attend. But now? As is? Not likely.

In current School practice elementary education is the first stage in a long heartbreaking series of waiting for something real to turn up — which never quite does. *Waiting for Godot* might be an allegory of American education. School is a place of marking time until the student can get out into a world where time is measured by experience that promises to relate more closely and meaningfully to his real life.

If the tension, pressure, anxiety, that is the price of staying in School resulted in a good start in life — the start of a good education — one might consider the price high but worth it. However, where the years of school are so painful, so long and so dull, and the end result so meager, this is not simply a high price to pay in the circumstances but a fraudulent one.

Triviality and superficiality suffocate the mind. The yawn is a gasp for living breath. No wonder School is notorious for smothering the desire to learn. Genuine education, the real article, is not mediocre, is not trivial, and is not dull.

The possibility ought not be entirely discounted that the classroom can be, not a Waiting Room but, as real a place as any other, providing that Education is the reality that the student encounters there.

The schools have learned the lesson all too well, that it is impractical to try to teach a child what is beyond his ability to learn. However, what the schools apparently have not learned is that it is also impractical to try to teach a child what is far below his ability to learn. The problem then becomes, How to keep him awake, or, How to keep him out of mischief, or How to keep him from breaking up the furniture. The mystery is not why children learn to read so badly in school, but why the continuing failure to teach reading well remains such a mystery.

The boring, wasteful, School years are destructive of the child's resources and of the nation's. A real educational system would go on the daring assumption that given something important to learn; given the teaching, discipline, language, necessary to learn it, Everychild would be found to have what it takes to be a learner.

The idea that the liberal arts are only important in the college years has the effect of drastically weakening their value even there. School students become college students without the necessary preparation.

In a real educational system, there would be enough and to spare of all the elements of education that are needed by all students, regardless of the variety and inequality of their gifts. And it would be the development of the respective gifts of all children— not merely or primarily the "academic type" — that would be of principal interest. There would, if anything, be a spirit that sees more occasion to rejoice for the education of one who was "lost" to learning, "and is found," than of one who "went not astray."

What resources would our schools need that they do not already have?

They now have the opportunity to teach young, impressionable minds, eager to learn (when they get them, in First Grade, at age six). They now have at least ten (compulsory) years in which to teach them. They now have, for the most part, the money for the physical facilities and resources with which to teach them.

But School does not know how to command its advantages. You could pump money into School from now till doomsday, but unless its nature were radically changed, it would not yield anything that seriously resembles Education.

Beyond a certain point, the more money that is poured into the schools, the worse they become. When the schools don't know the principle by which education proceeds, yet hope that by trial and error they might find it, this tends not only to be wasteful, expensive, and unproductive, but to have a confusing and adverse effect upon genuine education.

Some years ago the Evanston Township High School, in Illinois, "was voted No. 1 in America." according to a news story, by a national panel of educators. "Facilities include two swimming pools, a field house, a dozen gyms, a bank of computers, a 'journalistic suite' with $500,000 worth of equipment, including video tape recorders and a television studio." However, the article goes on, "students' difficulty in adjusting to the flexible scheduling has caused a rise in dropout, truancy and class-cutting this year..." A counselor in the school blames part of the problem on boredom, as do many of the students. "I don't know if we have enough resources," she said.

That School is compulsory is one of the central facts of the child's life. When his education goes wrong for him, a great chunk of his life goes wrong.

We may well ask ourselves, Why should a student trapped by School invest a great deal of himself in the trivial, the superficial, and the boring? In fact, how can he? Too little is there to invite a large investment. There's no real mystery as to why so many bright youngsters do so poorly in School. Giving little of themselves in these circumstances may be only a reasonable, instinctive, and practical economy of effort.

Most of us are unwilling or even unable to do our best in an environment that speaks to the least common denominator in us. Mediocrity is not inspiring.

That education must make sense to school students doesn't mean the Summerhill ("free school" or "open education") poppycock, popular in the sixties and seventies, that they should be allowed to determine substantive educational matters for themselves. The education of children is an adult responsibility. However, a coherent, rational plan of education is one that even a child would understand and appreciate. What child could possibly make educational sense out of the schools today? For that matter, what adult?

Summerhill was an educational backlash; it was a symbol of "freedom" and of everything diametrically opposed to the sterile, hated School system.

The subtitle of the book *Summerhill* is, *A Radical Approach to Child Rearing*. Child psychology, not education, is the main subject of this book. Its last section includes a topic, "About Learning" — one-and-a-half pages — which deals directly, though only in part, with the substance of education. This topic is included in the section "Question and Answers," the last question and answer of which are: Q. "What should a teacher do when a boy plays with his pencil when she is trying to teach a lesson?" — A. "Pencil equals penis. The boy has been forbidden to play with his penis. Cure: get the parents to take off the masturbation prohibition." The author, A. S. Neill, does not say what pencil equals — or what is the simple "cure" — when it is the teacher who plays with it.

However, our present school system is hateful not because it is restrictive, but because it is restrictive in a wasteful and meaningless way. The too little achievement to show for twelve or thirteen years spent there is not only restrictive but oppressive.

To learn a power of language is to acquire a discipline — which is restrictive but liberating. The student acquires a means to do or understand more than he could before of matters that enlarge his world, not constrict it.

Incompetence is a form of bondage, not freedom. A real education increases the power of the self in respect to the uses of language. It broadens the horizon and widens the scope of the world in which Everychild lives.

This kind of eduction is the golden mean between, on the one hand, School's meaningless restrictions and, on the other, the wasteful "freedom" of the Summerhill variety — which, because they do not educate, neither do they liberate.

Children cannot make important educational decisions for themselves — the important things to learn, the best means of learning them — because, as children, they cannot know where the centers of educational power are to be found; or, indeed, what is the use of finding them.

The genuine educator does know; or if in fact he does not, then he is no educator, whatever the title of his position may be. There is no substitute for the authority of the person or persons responsible for educating the child. If the educator — the teacher or the program itself — is not competent to educate, the children will not be educated.

It is difficult to avoid the suspicion that where everyone is being educated in "his own way," no one is being educated at all. We cannot ask the schools to tailor education to each individual child and at the same time hold them accountable for the "results." How would we know what results to look for, or how to evaluate them if everyone is being "educated" differently? Is there no elementary kind of education that would be good for every child?

Let freedom ring and diversity flourish. But also let a place be reserved for that of intelligence and imagination cultivated best in each only by being cultivated well in all. To look to a child, who knows little of either himself or the world, to be the architect of his own education is to guarantee that he will never be able to live well in the house of his own design.

The "free" school is the last refuge of the non-educator. If one does not know exactly what educational results are appropriate or how to achieve them or how to measure their achievement, he will naturally favor a system in which emphasis upon tangible results and specific competencies is made to seem authoritarian; either that or the meaning of this emphasis will be dissipated by the conviction that the results to be sought are "different" in each child and therefore presumably not measurable in each according to a common standard.

To insist that the schools be held accountable for clearly defined educational results and that students be held to high and objective criteria of achievement is not to insist upon measuring all performance by a grade. As we motivate, so shall we educate. If we do not corrupt every learning occasion by putting a price on it, the student just might respond to it freely, willingly, gladly.

There is no contradiction between, on the one hand, diminishing the importance of grades; and, on the other, raising standards. It will only seem so in a situation where grades are exorbitantly valued and educational standards are disgracefully low. One, not implausible, interpretation of the fact that so many students of high intelligence and high spirit either drop out of or do poorly in school is that grades seem to them so much of what School is all about, and they are looking for something better in life.

The student doesn't need to be an educational expert to discern that something is radically wrong with School. There are undoubtedly numerous reasons for his despair, but the principle of Ockham's razor eliminates the need to seek any further than the obvious one: School is an educational disaster.

No wonder the student quits when he can, no wonder his hostility shows. Not that the problem of youth in our society is purely and simply the fault of the schools. But School contributes more than its share to the heartache.

"I seemed to see an enormous school," writes Edwin Muir in his autobiography, "higher even than this one, and millions of children all over the world creeping toward it and disappearing into it...

"This was the feeling which my first year at school gave me, a feeling of being shut in some narrow, clean, wooden place; it must be known to everyone who has attended a school, and the volume of misery it has caused will not bear thinking of."

The mental suffering of others is difficult enough to see; but it is especially difficult for adults to perceive the agony of children who are victims of a bad educational system. The cause of their suffering is remote from adult experience; and thus, as it were, twice removed. The more painful the experience of childhood the more effectively the adult memory buries it. But no extended discussion of School that lacks reference to the unhappiness it causes can be said to touch its reality.

The failure of the schools is neither an accident nor evidence of villainy. One reason for it is simple. School lacks an understanding of the kind of education it should provide. School professionals give little or no sign of recognizing this, perhaps because they have been too readily persuaded by degrees, diplomas, credentials, and certificates, conferred upon them by like-minded and similarly-schooled conferees, attesting otherwise.

However, candor requires it also to be said, that even the good will of these scholastic leaders would be less open to question if they appeared more open to, and more competent to evaluate fairly, the serious criticism that has been levelled in recent decades against their theories and practices. If there is anything drastically wrong with American schools that money alone can do nothing about, these leaders do not see it.

There is no institution in our nation that has developed a more impervious skin to criticism or greater resistance to significant change — i.e. in the direction of Education — than School. School professionals will tell you a thousand reasons — when they are willing to admit any — for academic deficiencies of School, the most prominent of course being lack of money; but they are never willing to admit a single reason for which they are responsible

Understandably, members of the School establishment do not want the public "meddling" in educational matters. But just as understandably the public is not likely to become reconciled to the view that the failure of the schools is either inevitable, unimportant, or not its proper business.

"The intolerance of discussion and criticism." writes Frank MacKinnon, a Canadian educator, " on the part of educational administrators in both Canada and the United States has assumed the proportions of a national scandal. It is almost without parallel in the entire structure of government. Most politicians and civil servants expect discussion and criticism as a matter of course....In education, however, there is no real opportunity for constructive criticism to be brought to bear on the administration."

A layman who criticizes the schools on matters of educational significance is said to be Attacking Public Education. A teacher who criticizes them on the same grounds is said to be Intellectualizing — or worse. The schools are hostile both to external and to internal criticism. It took a Supreme Court decision in 1968 (Pickering v. Lockport Township) to establish that a public school teacher may not be discharged for criticism of public school officials.

Because there is lacking in the schools any agreement upon what kind of education is of most worth, intellectual anarchy reigns there. To be sure, more educational "philosophy" is to be found in School environs than any philosophically-inclined, theoretically-minded, madcap could possibly require. Unfortunately, no matter how one slices this philosophy, it is usually found to be School, not Education.

Schooling is notoriously hard for the public to remedy. No one loses his property or goes to jail as its immediate result. Only a child's imagination suffers, only his intelligence is imprisoned. The condition of American education today is like that of a patient whose skin is so extensively burned that there is little left of it to graft. Who will educate the educators? Parents, for the most part, cannot take their childrens' education into their own hands. What would they do with it once it gets there? A parent may have no better understanding of the educational needs of his child than a school official, but his concern is naturally greater because it is his child whom School is failing.

The Doctor of Education is the chief of the School establishment. His philosophy of education is manifest in the laws that control the curriculum, control the certification of personnel, control selection of learning materials — control, in other words, the commanding heights. (More doctorates in education are granted in this country each year than in any other subject.)

This Doctor is the "expert" of American education. The School ethos is his creation He is the professor of education, the superintendent of schools, the commissioner of the state department of education, the dean or president of the community college, the executive secretary of the state education association, the bureau chief of the U. S. Department of Education — the principal officer and architect of the present educational farrago in the United States.

It would not be generous to expatiate upon the place held by the intellectual accomplishments of these Doctors in the general estimate of the world of learning. But the schools do reflect — in theory and practice, in spirit and methods — the intellectual quality of their leaders. And if it be the surest sign of stupidity that the intelligence of others is consistently downgraded, then it must be said, generous or not, that the schools, which so devastatingly downgrade the learning capabilities of their students, do not accidentally reflect the intelligence of these leaders.

"It is these experts," writes James D. Koerner (in *Who Controls American Education?*), "sharing much the same background and outlook and having been through homogeneous training programs for advanced degrees in schools of education, who lay claim to special knowledge that is supposed to distinguish them from 'the rest of us'. It has been out of deference to this specialized knowledge that the rest of us have allowed the expert to exert as much control as he now does over educational policy.

"If I could leave the reader with only one impression in this book, I would like him to take away the conviction that all of us have badly over-estimated the quality and extent of expert knowledge in education."

One would never question the ability of these Doctors to supervise other Doctors. One would appoint them to administer provinces. In the learning institutions run by these Doctors, the grass gets mowed and the plumbing works. They are admirably efficient in grades, units, degrees, diplomas, and average daily attendance reports. It is only intelligence and imagination that do not flourish under their administration. "We cannot avoid adopting the belief," said Plato, "that the real nature of education is at variance with the account given of it by certain of its professors." How these Doctors became educational chiefs without first mastering traditional fields of learning is a paradox held by them as too profound for lay intelligence.

Nevertheless, it must also be said, that to be well-educated doesn't necessarily guarantee a cogent understanding of education, as is illustrated by the following passage from a letter by Aldous Huxley, who was considered one of the best educated men of his time. "My own feeling is that, if we could combine Krishnamurti with old Dr. Vittoz's brand of psychotherapy and F. M. Alexander's method of 'creative conscious control' of posture and bodily function, with a bit of general semantics thrown in to help us steer clear of verbal and conceptual pitfalls, and a sensible diet, we would have solved the problem of preventative medicine and, along with it, at least half the problem of education." And in another letter, Huxley writes: "Is it too much to hope that a system of education may some day be devised [in which]...mescaline or some other chemical substance may play a part by making it possible for young people to 'taste and see' what they have learned about at second hand, or directly but at a lower level of intensity, in the writings of the religious, or the works of poets, painters and musicians?"

It may be that fewer professional chiefs and more amateur indians are just what are required to redress the situation. To be an amateur has both pejorative and honorific connotation. An amateur loves and is absorbed in his subject, is not paid for thinking about it, and speaks with no external authority respecting it.

The main dynamic of educational change will have to come from those indians finally responsible — the American people. It will take more than money to do it. It will take understanding of what ought to be changed; understanding, in brief, of what constitutes a good education. Everychild will get the kind of education that Everyman enables him to get.

How is the present abysmal state of education in the schools to be raised to a state of excellence? How, in brief, can American schooling become American education?

"The public schools we have today are what the powerful and considerable have made of them." ("Why Johnnie Can't Think," by Walter Karp, *Harper's*, June 1985) The implication is that the economically privileged are the ones responsible; that there is some kind of conspiracy afoot to keep the pupils from lower income levels down in order to reserve for pupils from upper middle income families subjects of academic value; that children of the poor are deliberately shunted into vocational courses and those of the more affluent into college-oriented subjects.

For a variety of reasons, pupils from poor families do indeed fare less well in school than the pupils from economically advantaged backgrounds. But the fact of the matter is, that our schools are not poor because of a conspiracy of the rich or because of being inadequately funded. They are poor because, quite simply, they do not know how to educate. They lack a valid philosophy of education. They lack the intellectual— not economic — means to achieve the appropriate objective: namely, the education of Everychild. School professionals are degreed; they are diplomed; they are certificated; they are conferenced and workshopped. But they are not educated. How, then, is it possible for them to educate?

The public demands that children receive the fundamentals of an authentic education. But the public doesn't know any better than the schools how to do this. They do know, however, that it isn't being done now — which is, apparently, more than the schools know, or want to know.

Let a school be assumed in which from the first day in the First Grade the student's time is used to maximum advantage.

Respect for his intelligence, imagination, and personal dignity is implicit in its curriculum, in its methods of instruction, in the education of its teachers, and in the quality of its learning materials.

The aim of the curriculum is to nurture his intelligence and imagination and to teach him the skills and art of language that will be of greatest value to him all his life, which generate the most effective kinds of understanding and competence.

He is learning to read well for his age (having been taught the rudiments with a phonetic method and continued with the best of children's literature); learning to speak and read a foreign language; acquiring the fundamentals of a sound musical education (as a performer) and visual art education (as a craftsman); studying history, science and mathematics as liberal arts.

Liberal artists or good craftsmen in all these subjects are his teachers. He doesn't want to drop out or inwardly withdraw from this kind of education because it uses him well. He is interested in what he is learning; and, because the program is readily intelligible, he gains an increasing understanding of its rationale as he participates in it. He is embarked upon the first stage of a liberal education.

What parents would not want this kind of education for their boy or girl, if they could get it?

Chapter III

OPENING TO THE LIGHT:
ON THE IDEA OF ELEMENTARY EDUCATION

> The intelligence can only be led by desire. For there to be desire, there
> must be pleasure and joy in the work....The joy of learning is as
> indispensable in study as breathing is in running. Where it
> is lacking, there are no real students, but only poor
> caricatures of apprentices who at the end of their
> apprenticeship, will not even have a trade.
>
> SimoneWeil

How large is the problem of American education? Forty five million children? Three million teachers? Fifteen thousand school districts? Two hundred billion dollars? Not at all. It is the size of one ordinary human intelligence, but that's fairly large; it is the size of one ordinary human imagination, but that's even larger; it is the size of one ordinary human spirit, but that's immeasurable.

The elementary education proposed here for all children might also be thought of as a pattern for the education of one child — not a moron, not a genius; but a child of ordinary intelligence, a "typical" boy or girl. Everychild.

The intelligence of the child one must have in mind in prescribing an elementary education for all children is described as "ordinary" only in the sense of being fairly representative of the population at his age level and for the purpose of acquiring the best possible elementary education that he can; ordinary rather than "average," which suggests a statistical view that blunts the idea of the individual person, and rather than "normal," which connotes irrelevancies (for this purpose) of mental health.

The education that we envision for this ordinary child should be, by current standards, extraordinary.

Neither Everychild nor his parents have any desire to see him as the main character in an educational fiction series: Why Everychild Can't Learn Mathematics, Why Everychild Can't Learn Music, Why Everychild Can't Learn Visual Art, Why Everychild Can't Learn to Read or Write, Why Everychild Can't Learn a Foreign Language. (The entire series titled: Why Everychild Can't Learn Academic Subjects).

They think that it is not helpful to demean his potentialities. They think that there is no way of knowing what effect the best kind of education — and they want the best — might have upon him: how it might develop observable powers or reveal hidden ones. They have heard of the wonders that the right kind of education has effected in even the most seemingly hopeless of children. However, they know that it is not the most seemingly hopeless whom the schools are commissioned to educate but the most seemingly ordinary.

Every child is more likely to be found educable when his intelligence is not held cheaply and when serious means are employed to educate him. Tests that presume to add him up and fix his capabilities for learning, like some kind of race track odds, not only demean him but demean the very idea of intelligence, which, particularly in children, doesn't lend itself well either to quantitative measurement or to the predictions that such measurement supposedly validates.

It is as true that a student of ordinary intelligence is capable of acquiring the rudiments of a liberal education as it is that a democratic society has crucial need for liberally educated citizens.

Elementary education as here defined is the most important part of the entire educational system. It is the initial, academic study whose deficiencies are most crippling and whose competencies are most strengthening to the other parts.

It is the beginning of the formal study of language.

It is the introduction to a heritage whose old masters are the Old Masters and whose new masters have their roots in that tradition.

There is no more effective introduction to education that by means of works that powerfully express the nature of language.

Of course it is possible to introduce a child incompetently to language; it is possible to enable him to catch occasional glimpses of the real thing, but not the steady vision of its power. It is also curious and pathetic, that with much effort, with much good will, with much money, this is what in fact School does.

Elementary education is taught in the schools by poorly educated teachers, with the worst books, in the most wasteful, meaningless, and ill-conceived curriculum, of the entire educational enterprise

The years of waste and boredom that attend the School experience for most children are not written in their contract with life as a matter of necessity. It could be made to happen otherwise.

What motivates learning most effectively?

In Coleridge's "Rime of the Ancient Mariner" the Wedding Guest is not only held by the mariner's glittering eye, but also "he cannot choose but hear" because the intrinsic interest of the story holds him spellbound.

A wise teacher will know how to make use of the ways in which the intrinsic interest of the work in hand invokes the corresponding interest of the student. There is an integral link between the willingness of a student to invest his attention in reading a good book and the extent to which a good book possesses the power to justify his investment.

The best works for educational purposes are those that engage the intelligence and imagination of the student at the deepest and highest levels, to justify the fullest attention. They are also occasions of curiosity and wonder because our interpretations of them do not — cannot — exhaust their meaning.

A good book both seduces and compels the reader to a more intense interest than an "entertainment," although this is not to say that the best books may not be entertaining — that is, provide "pleasure and joy in the work," as Simone Weil says in the quotation at the head of this chapter.

The quality of attention a work induces is one index of its intrinsic interest; but not, however, an only or infallible one. Because there is no infallible judgment in this realm, no work in the curriculum should be considered above reconsideration and re-evaluation. But who cannot think of works of art whose enduring reputation appears fairly secure?

If a good or great book is more likely to engage the interest of the student and encourage a greater investment of his intelligence than a poor one, why are the books used in the schools almost invariably so poor? What does School know about the educational benefit of School textbooks that escapes the supposedly inexpert, unqualified, non-professional understanding?

Providing the fundamentals of a genuine education for all is within the realm of the practicable. However, these fundamentals are not what the theory and practice of the schools now take them to be.

There is no more urgent educational task confronting our society at the present time than to re-define this first decisive part of education and to re-organize the educational system accordingly.

It is the enduring that education needs. The ruling passion of a system of education must be its thirst for the first-rate.

The deterioration of learning that appears so scandalous when revealed on the college and graduate school levels didn't begin there. If we want to improve the quality of education in our colleges and universities, we must begin with the schools.

The present intellectual shambles of the university and of the college suggests that we do not know what "higher" education is or ought to be. It also suggests that neither do we know what "lower" or elementary education is or ought to be. The only meaning of higher education — as distinct from vocational or professional training — that makes any sense is as a continuation of the elements of education well begun in the schools.

Great art, seminal ideas, fundamental questions — these are the primary substance of lower education, of higher education, and, one supposes, of continuing education for a lifetime.

It is a truism, that if we would take the idea of democracy seriously, we must take education seriously. It should be just as self-evident that if we would take education seriously, we must begin in the First Grade.

The first ten years of study in the fundamentals of learning are the years of elementary education, no matter what the building is called in which it occurs. Of what educational significance is it whether the curriculum is sliced on an 8-4, 6-3-3, 4-3-3-2, or other such numerical basis? Grade school, junior high school, high school — what is all this but *elementary* education?

There are only the elements of education to be acquired in childhood and adolescent years. Because School has no significant form, one part bears no intelligible relation to another. Disjunction of the curriculum at the school level anticipates its departmental division at the college level.

One unified course of study that taught elementary educational disciplines to Everychild could be given in the ten-year period from age six to sixteen. After that, whether or not additional study of this kind would be possible, necessary, or desirable, depends upon the particular student and the opportunities afforded him.

At sixteen young people feel at a crossroad in their lives. They have discovered enough of their capabilities and ambitions to make a provisional decision as to whether or not they want to pursue further academic studies. At this age a youth would be ready, under the plan proposed here, either to learn a marketable skill or to go on to higher education.

If he decided to pursue additional years of education in college, and had the ability and interest for it, he would be intellectually prepared to do so. In college he would be deepening and broadening the same kind of studies already well begun. Whether or not he went on to college and further liberal learning, he could be confident that he had at least travelled the beginning of the right road. He would not have to spend the rest of his life either regretting all that he should have learned in school but didn't, or going over and over the same ground, looking for the place his education first got lost.

Underneath those cheerful, well-scrubbed, healthy, attractive faces of American school children is the confusion not merely of childhood and adolescence, but of being caught up in an educational unworld, in which, for some, drugs, alcohol, and sex appear to them the only way out. Our present School chowchow is much more successful in the prevention of education than in its achievement.

Here is a young man who has just received his Bachelor of Arts degree from a well-known university. He is twenty-two years old and has been engaged in academic study for the past sixteen years.

Can he read, write, or speak his native tongue with the competence reasonably expected from all those years of study? No.

Does he have a reasonable competence in mathematics and comprehension of some of its major ideas? No.

Does he have proficiency in, or more than the merest smattering about, musical or visual art? No.

Does he know much science worth knowing? No.

Does he have the knowledge of history, economics, and political institutions reasonably to be expected of a citizen in a democratic republic? No.

How is this young man going to earn his living? He is going to be a school teacher (and, later on, a school principal; and after that superintendent of schools — with a doctorate of course in education).

Many college and university teachers complain about their students—their reading ability, their writing ability, their thinking ability, their general lack of interest in learning.

But it's not surprising that, if students come to college with twelve years of poor schooling as preparation, they should be poor students. Blaming their students for this condition is blaming the victims for the crime.

Furthermore, how much better than the schools are the colleges in providing a decent education for their students?

How well qualified is a student with poor preparation for college to make up the substance and structure of his college curriculum?

How good an education does a college provide that requires of their students little more than attendance at lectures, and grades them on how well they are able to regurgitate the contents thereof? that grants a degree to a student who may never have been required to read, discuss, and think about a great book, or to learn a foreign language with a reasonable competence in reading, writing, and speaking it (Never mind their competence to do the same with their native tongue.), or to evidence a basic knowledge of, or ability to use, visual art, music, mathematics and science, history and government?

Is it really any wonder when college in its turn and according to its particular mission and responsibility is hardly any better than school, that graduate schools and departments should complain in their turn of how poor their students are?

The parent who feels that he has good reason to be dissatisfied with the education of his children in the schools may wish, like Grangousier, Gargantua's father, to conclude that it were better for his son "to learn nothing at all, than to be taught such-like books, under such schoolmasters."

Grangousier reaches this unhappy conclusion after his son has been studying for a while with one Master Jobeline Bridé, "or muzzled dolt." It was not that Gargantua had no aptitude for learning but that "although he spent all his time in it, he did nevertheless profit nothing, but which is worse grew thereby foolish, simple, doted and blockish...."

In order to learn how miserable his son had been educated, Grangousier arranged a speech contest between Gargantua and a young page of a nearby court. The page delivered his address "with such proper gestures, such distinct pronunciation, so pleasant a delivery, in such exquisite fine terms, and so good Latin, that he seemed rather a Gracchus, a Cicero, an Aemilius of the past, than a youth of his age. But all the countenance that Gargantua kept was, that he fell to crying like a cow, and cast down his face, hiding it with his cap, nor could they possibly draw one word from him, no more than a fart from a dead ass. Whereat his father was so grievously vexed that he would have killed Master Jobeline...." He was withheld from these murderous inclinations, with which any American parent might sympathize, "by fair persuasions, so that at length he pacified his wrath."

Grangousier was a wise and loving father, who did not think that his child was a "non-academic type." When the teacher was dismissed and the method of instruction changed, Gargantua was discovered to be marvelously educable. But first he had to be cleansed of all the "perverse habitude of his brain." Rabelais tells us that, "To do this better, they brought him into the company of learned men, which were there, in whose imitation he had a great desire and affection to study otherwise, and to improve his parts. Afterwards he put himself into such a road and way of studying that he lost not any hour in the day, but employed all his time in learning, and honest knowledge."

Who can say what would be Everychild's talent for learning and honest knowledge once he were brought into the company of learned men, either directly or as represented in their works?

A sound educational economy would know how to make effective use of the fact that, although good teachers are at a premium, there is an inexpensive and inexhaustible supply of good books. However, it should not be assumed that the number of good teachers available at any one time is a fixed quantity. Much depends upon the quality of intelligence and imagination looked for in the teaching faculty. Much depends also upon the educational aims for which prospective teachers are sought, and whether their powers to teach and to learn will be well used.

The best teachers are those who ask the best questions; the best questions are those that in discussion are directed toward the best understanding of the work in hand; and the best works are those that raise in the most notable way the most important questions.

(The definition of certain terms that have an essential use in education — and, indeed, in life — like "best," "important," "first-rate," "great," invariably involves other terms that require further defining. "We cannot find words," writes Elizabeth Hardwick, "except in tautology, for the power of splendid creations." But an even worse dilemma than that involved in the use of these imperfectly defined and imperfectly applied terms is that of failing to make the essential judgments that require their use.)

A good teacher knows that he must not come between a good book and its reader, except as strictly necessary. In general, it may be safely assumed that the author of a good or great book knows better than the teacher, the critic, or the State curriculum commission, what he wants to say and how he wants to say it. If benevolent and fortuitous circumstances have put a good book into the student's hand, the kindest, most courteous, most loving deed that the teacher can perform toward both author and reader is not to corrupt the communication between them with "interpretations."

A good teacher knows this. He knows that if it is a good book, the assumption is fair that his presence is an intrusion until proven otherwise. It is possible for him to get past this initial bar to his entrance, but only by asking the right questions. This assumption is a sphinx that requires questions, not answers.

The role of the discussion leaders, says the *Catalog* of St. John's College (Annapolis, Md., Santa Fe, N.M.) "is not to give information, nor is it to produce the 'right' opinion or interpretation. It is to guide the discussion, to keep it moving, to raise objections, to help the student in every way possible to understand the author, the issues, and himself. The most useful instrument for this purpose is the question; perhaps the most useful device of all is the question 'Why?' But a leader may also take a definite and positive stand and enter directly into the argument. If he does so, however, he can expect no special consideration. Reason is the only recognized authority; all opinions must be rationally defended and any single opinion can prevail only by general consent. The aim is always to develop the student's powers of reason and understanding and to help him arrive at intelligent opinions of his own."

The best questions are those whose answers are not likely to be found in a moment, or even in a day or a year, possibly not even in a lifetime.

If a sound curriculum will generally eschew books that are not worth reading even once; so, too, it will generally decline to concern itself much with questions that are simply answered, once and for all.

Education is a place to learn to question the answers, as well as to question the questions. It is a place to learn to entertain the right doubts.

Questioning to the point, questioning the how or why of anything that is alive enough to matter — good teaching hardly consists of more than this. "Reflective thinking," wrote John Dewey, "involves (1) a state of doubt...and (2) an act of searching...."

If there is any one truth that Socrates is intent upon teaching, it is that those who have no doubt about what they know, or think they know, are unteachable. "The wise," said Plato, "are full of doubt." And elsewhere, in the *Meno*, Socrates declares: "I perplex others, not because I am clear, but because I am utterly perplexed myself." This might be considered another instance of Socratic irony. But if a road to understanding and knowledge does not begin with ignorance and perplexity, what would be the reason for taking it?

Questions are symptoms of doubt that invite participation and stimulate interest. Answers settle the matter — as often as not, to a premature conclusion. Questions assume that the limits of understanding have not been reached: they seek the increase. A teacher cannot provide a better example of a learner to his students than by questions that enlarge the scope of meaning.

That this is not a description of common pedagogical practice will come as news to no one. "Tis the custom of pedagogues," writes Montaigne, "to be eternally thundering in their pupils' ears, as they were pouring into a funnel while the business of the pupil is only to repeat what the others have said...." Regurgitation, not education. In Montaigne's age, before printed books were generally available, there was a more legitimate excuse for the lecture as a method of teaching than there is today when the printed book enables and indeed invites a teacher to be, not the primary source of illumination but, a way to better understanding of a primary source.

The teacher justifies his presence on the scene by asking questions that better enable his students to understand the work under discussion. The alternative is to pretend to an authority he does not have. He lectures. The students ask questions of him. He answers these confidently, as an academic virtuoso should. He has no serious perplexities, so there need be no "act of searching"; and of course no occasion for "reflective thinking."

In discussing a first-rate book with his students, the teacher who knows enough to know that he is, or should be, in a state of some doubt raised by a careful and honest reading of it will engage his students in a common quest by putting questions pertinent to this state, and so open to them a way to participate responsibly in the act of searching. He will raise questions of interpretation that might be asked of the author if he were present.

There is, however, nothing to prevent an addiction to certitude from controlling the ways of inquiry also. It is possible to be as dogmatic in questioning as in lecturing. Certitude wears various masks. The spirit is what counts: it is the spirit of doubt, of inquiry, of openness, of flexibility, of humility, of courtesy, that serves truth.

Certitudes tend to crack under fire when they have not first been tested by radically honest doubt. A passion for truth must be tempered by an assumption of human fallibility in knowing it. The ways of inquiry that are not rooted in honest doubt may be only a more subtle kind of certitude.

Discussion requires the teacher to be related to his students in a radically different way from the lecture method — a difference that evidences itself physically as well as psychologically. In discussion the teacher and all the students confront each other about the table or rectangle of tables, and the teacher is as much engaged in the search for meaning as his students. He is no Mark Hopkins; he is not there as an authority; he is there to lead a Query and a Quest. But it must be genuine discussion, motivated by genuine doubt, not one rigged to an inevitable conclusion.

The discussion of a book is a good way to tell how well it has been read. Is the class being held to a close reading of what the author says, and to a reasonable interpretation of what he means? Are the participants required to interpret before being permitted to evaluate? Are they required to follow the argument in a rational manner? Is there vitality in the discussion? Is the discussion disciplined? Is it free? Are the students learning to be better listeners and speakers as well as better readers?

"All the great arts," said Plato, "require discussion." Good discussion clarifies and deepens the encounter. It is as intrinsic to liberal education as great works of art themselves.

Discussion is a place where the student is spoken with, not to. In listening and speaking the way is open for him to be a person, not a sounding board. A good discussion provides the opportunity for "the meeting-place of various modes of imagining."

In learning how to participate in a discussion, the students should be taught: (1) to listen to others as carefully as they would be listened to; (2) to speak to others as though their desire to listen and to understand were at least as earnest as one's own; and (3) to assume that the need of the others to achieve a truer understanding of the text and of the questions based upon it is a like need to one's own.

Discussion *per se* is no sure cure. A poor discussion can be a deadly bore and a good lecture a lively engagement of ideas. However, in general, discussion is not only the method more favorable to education than any other; discussion at best is education at its best. It is not only a way of learning, but also a way of being.

There are four major "languages" of human communication: the language of words, the language of mathematics, the language of visual art, and the language of music. A student who has acquired understanding and competence in their use may still be an innocent in the world of learning, but he will not be an alien. In these four languages, man's intelligence and imagination create and have created the substance of liberal education.

Liberal arts are the native powers of language. The liberal arts that belong to each of these languages of learning on their elementary and fundamental levels are the powers that are peculiar to each of them. In the language of words: reading, writing, speaking, and listening; in the language of mathematics: the computational skills and conceptual powers (e.g., arithmetic and geometry); in the language of visual art: observing, seeing, interpreting and transforming; in the language of music: performing in rhythm and with good quality of tone, and, above all, listening.

The *trivium* (grammar, rhetoric, and logic) and the *quadrivium* (arithmetic, music, geometry, and astronomy) were what measured and recorded the world of meaning for the ancient and medieval eras. These seven liberal arts served Western culture as the curriculum of liberal education for more than a millennium and a half. But "The arts that liberate and humanize," declared Professor Richard P. McKeon, "must be constituted anew, as they have been reconstituted to meet new problems at various periods of their past. Their history suggests that a new formulation of the arts must be based on examination of the subject matters with which they must be concerned and of the disciplines which are adopted to accomplish their liberal and humane purposes." Language — and our conception of it — changes. Music is not primarily understood in our age as a branch of mathematics, nor should visual art be excluded from the arts whose purposes are "liberal and humane." The languages of learning are fundamental to liberal education in three principal ways.

First, each has its own distinct notation. By means of their written — or, in visual art, plastic — record, they free us from a total dependence upon the present. They function as both telescope and microscope, enabling us to take not only a closer view of past ages but also a longer view of the present. They are also a kind of balance, extending over thousands of years of human culture.

Secondly, each of these languages has its own principles of meaning and integrity. The liberal arts are the rational foundations and the effective techniques that distinguish each language when used at its best. They are the criteria that measure the quality of language. They are ways of feeling, thinking about, imagining, and preserving the account of experience that matters.

Thirdly, each of the four languages is a vehicle for individual genius. "The first step towards understanding the integrity of art," wrote the noted music critic Donald Francis Tovey, " is to recognize that it consists in the integrity of each individual work of art;...there is no such thing as Art with a capital A." We cannot even know the integrity of the workmanship and technique of art except as these are manifest in an individual work; and it is in the individual work — and its relation to other individual works — that art evidences itself to future generations as unmistakably as to its own.

There is an issue between the artist and his world, between him and the tradition of his art, between him and all the influences of his life that have had their way with him, willingly or not. His work proclaims how things stand here, in the mind and heart of this person, however they may appear somewhere else. But he does not only speak for himself. "There's no offense, my Lord." — Yes, by Saint Patrick, but there is, Horatio, and much offense too."

Because there is offense and because it takes courage and honesty and strength to declare it effectively, nations honor their artists — when they do not fear, revile, and persecute them.

Out of the appearance of things, art composes a reality of its own that in some mysterious way coincides with a reality that is not its own. Composition is the proof that within the limits of his work the artist has taken charge with authority.

But of what does he take charge?

Art is a means of discovering something greater than itself — reality, beauty, life. It is a reflected glory. It discovers something greater when it has been true to its own reality, when it has first gained mastery over itself.

The artist is no conqueror, but he is a sovereign in his own realm. He paints, he writes, he composes — these are his realms. But he is also a refugee and a supplicant. This is a weak and foolish king; this is a Lear. And the world, like Lear's elder daughters, is nothing if not down-to-earth.

> For poetry makes nothing happen: it survives
> In a valley of its saying where executives
> Would never want to tamper; it flows south
> From ranches of isolation and the busy griefs,
> Raw towns that we believe and die in; it survives,
> A way of happening, a mouth. (W. H. Auden)

The Fool understood the agony of a powerless kingship. Humor helped, irony helped. He knew a fellow-artist when he saw one.

Art was not a palace but a hovel into which only fools crept: a king on his way to madness and death, a naked beggar who kept his life only by pretending to have lost his reason, and — a Fool.

What a company! Artists all. Each either mad or feigning a part — to be more true.

The academician, the culture operator, the foundation man, the patronizer of the arts, are not tempted to take the chances that the radical query and quest of art must take. Not a fool in a carload.

An artist discovers in his work what his work is, where in life to risk his life. He hasn't begun with an idea and drawn its logical conclusion. He has begun with an illogical unconclusion — himself — and there broken through, like Lear, to his real kingdom.

Education is no more a success story than art. Based on art, how should it be? The art of education holds out to the learner the same chance as the artists whose works he studies: of discovering what he can mean and what he can know and a way to venture what is crucial.

The education of Everychild must proceed continuously along both horizontal and vertical lines. He gains new knowledge at the same time and in the same way that he acquires a deepening of what he already knows.

The forms of language are studied best in the examples of each that are fundamental, both in the sense of being primary and in the sense of being directed to the matters that matter, and that do so memorably. "The desire to improve our reading," writes I. A. Richards, "worthy though it is, won't help us unless it operates through the work of puzzling out a passage because we care what it says." Our caring what it says (and the child is surely no different from the adult in this) is not unrelated to the substance of what it says and to the style in which it says it.

Is the style the book? No, it is only one of its signatures. Yes, by its style it is most recognizable. Style is an extension of its power.

We tend, naturally, to think of what is fundamental in the vertical perspective as belonging to the latter stages of education; indeed, to the latter stages of life. How could the values and achievements that belong to the fundamentals of learning in its vertical perspective be construed as an integral and essential part of its beginning stage? It is, after all, an educational philosophy for children that is being expounded here.

If wisdom seems an extravagant term for the aim of learning at the elementary stage, and if this aim is not yet in the child, then let us hope that one day it may be and let us do what we can to advance him toward it.

To help cultivate the deeper levels of intelligence in the student should not be irrelevant to any stage of the learning process. It is only a recognition of his humanity. Even children are intelligent beings. The fruits of their intelligence may be just as rarely evidenced as its incidence in their elders. It is not a fixed point on the horizon that we reach or approach only in middle or old age, but a quality of spirit that reveals itself at any time and at any age.

The deeper levels of a child's understanding can and should be recognized, addressed, responded to, wakened. The knowledge that can be taught a child, and his power to understand it in a context shaped by time, experience, sorrow, shame, authority — all the major experiences of life — are not yet one in him. When he becomes a man, when he knows what he knows — and is at least party suspicious of it — they will be, and the strength of his humanity the proof.

The educational system that neglects the deeper ground of the child's understanding will fail to cultivate even the surface properly. The intelligence of the child ought to be engaged by the kind of learning that encompasses them both as part of the same experience.

Whatever we would have students achieve at the end of the curriculum, we ought to help them achieve in due measure at the beginning and all the rest of the way.

We usually assume that the schools can do something about the cultivation of intelligence, but that if they do no injury to the child's imagination that is about as much as can be hoped. However, the distinction between intelligence and imagination is more easily made by definition than description. We lack a single word that expresses their integral functioning.

A better understanding of intelligence must include imagination as a part of it. How is it possible to be intelligent, lacking imagination; or imaginative, unintelligently? One would be hard put to it to find any work of art (or, for that matter, any significant human activity) in which both intelligence and imagination do not function together.

The school economy that doesn't know how to teach a student to use his reason well will naturally squander his imaginative powers also, and the conditions of learning that are favorable to the one will naturally be favorable to the other also.

The art of imagination is to Posit Otherwise. It is to worry Certitude, which may look impregnable enough until some bold and imaginative fellow comes along and pushes it a little. "The best minds," wrote Robert Frost, "are those best at premises." Standing an hypothesis upon its head and discovering it to be even more consistent with reality that way is not only creative but exhilarating.

Imagination proposes possible worlds that illuminate a real one; it is a means intelligence uses to extend itself. Trusting of facts but suspicious of imagination is not an environment in which intelligence thrives. A purely factual view of the world is necessarily flat.

Let those responsible for the education of a child give him their confidence and support. Let them respect his pride and trust his honor. Let them bring him up in a direction that is upward for him. Pettiness and triviality weigh him down. He will rise better if buoyant.

The depth of personal sovereignty, the loneliness of the long distance runner, are instinctively hostile to the indignities of didacticism and moralistic injunction; "objective" tests and measurements; uncritical formulae, exercises, and manipulations; continual grading and competition for grades; gratuitous psychoanalyses— all such trickery-jobbery, no matter how well-intentioned and determined upon Everychild's welfare they represent themselves.

It should, at best, be the deeper ground of the child's understanding that education aims to cultivate, but not the deepest. The ultimate wilderness area of his life is not the proper concern of any educational system.

He needs freedom to breathe — not pure freedom, which is toxic, but an even mixture. Ah, who knows all he needs? Part must be left only for him, part only for God, to know.

Chapter IV
THE AIMS OF EDUCATION:
A PHILOSOPHY OF RESTRAINT

> Elementary education can do nothing better for a child than store
> his memory with things deserving to be there. He will be grateful
> for them when he grows up, even if he kicks now. They should
> be good things; indeed, they should be the best things,
> and all children should possess them.
>
> Mark Van Doren

The belief that education is the shortest line between vice and virtue is civilized man's perennial, and one of his most powerful, illusions. The temptation to assume that a life of intellectual activity must result in a good life is often greater than those who pursue intellectual activities can easily resist. The celebration of cerebration or contemplation is not necessarily the highest wisdom; THINK, not the world's most inspiring slogan. "A man can read and read and read and think and think and still be a villain...."

Nor is human goodness guaranteed by how well a man reads or how profoundly he thinks. The learned are as much inclined toward self-aggrandizement, self-justification, self-indulgence, self-absorption, self-serving, self-deception, as any other privileged group.

If philosophers of education are usually more prone to assume the goodness and perfectibility of human nature than are novelists and dramatists, this may be because writers of fiction are obliged to portray particular characters convincingly. Understanding life's little problems on the one hand, and resolving them justly and lovingly in the fabric of one's own life and community on the other are, as most of us at least suspect, two radically different propositions.

A man might be the greatest poet, philosopher, or philanthropist of his age and the question would still be relevant: What kind of man is he?

The art of eduction does not consist, as may be supposed, in knowing which strings need only be touched for the student to resound virtue. What illumines the mind doesn't necessarily make the learner pure in heart or hunger and thirst after righteousness.

In the Introduction to Rilke's *Selected Works*, J. B. Leishman, commenting upon the translator, G. Craig Houston, observes: "She attached, as I have said, much importance to the cultivation of insight and perception, which were her special gifts, and Rilke's innumerable insights and perceptions and his most subtle, delicate and original expression of them enabled her to extend the depth and range of her own. For this she was grateful, and expected other readers to be grateful. But for the right use of these acquisitions, as of all other gifts, natural or acquired, for their relation to the whole duty of man, for their place and important *sub specie aeternitatis* — she knew that neither Rilke nor any other poet could teach her that, and she often became impatient with those who expected to learn from poets what they should have learned at their mothers's knee, or to find in poets a substitute for what each must work out with fear and trembling for himself."

Although education can teach the student to read and interpret the languages of learning and to use them with some degree of competence — and to this extent take him in the right direction — it cannot warrant that he will be able to transmute these achievements into other kinds of honest existence.

The greatest president in the history of the Republic contributed more to our understanding of the nature of democratic government by the quality of his character, as he revealed it in personal life and in political activity, than by his contributions to its democratic theory.

What we learn from Lincoln about the idea of democracy depends not a little upon the fact that it is Lincoln from whom we learn it.

That education is not an unmitigated blessing probably first occurred to Adam upon being ejected from the Garden of Eden for eating of the tree of the knowledge of good and evil.

"The aims of education," wrote the late Robert M. Hutchins, one of the most eminent twentieth century American spokesmen for liberal education, "appear to be understanding, to know the reason for things." This would appear to be a good enough reason for wanting it. But if "Education is hard to measure," as Mr. Hutchins also says, it is, as he does not say, impossible to evaluate in terms of its subsequent moral fruits.

When he goes on to declare that: "Education is the process of learning to lead the good life. The permanence of the good habits that are formed by good acts, that induce further good acts, and so constitute a good life, is guaranteed by an intellectual grasp of the aims of life and of the means of achieving them." — this is somewhat less persuasive. It is a long way from the premise that education increases our understanding to the conclusion that a good life is "guaranteed by an intellectual grasp of the aims of life." The freedom of the self can out-wit its education every time*

---

*Although Robert Hutchins had an exaggerated notion of what education could accomplish for the redemption of the individual and of the social order, he and Mortimer J. Adler, who was an associate of Hutchins at The University of Chicago, contributed the most interesting and significant philosophy of education in this century, whose "great books" teachings were clearly influential in the writing of this book, and hereby gratefully acknowledged.

Knowledge of the idea of virtue may be helpful to its realization in practice, but it is hardly sufficient. "We men," wrote Kierkegaard ... "have concentrated our whole attention upon understanding and knowing; we pretend that it is here the difficulty lies, and that then the consequence naturally follows that if only we understand what is right, it then follows as a matter of course that we would do it. Oh, tragic misunderstanding, or cunning invention! No, infinitely farther than from the profoundest ignorance to the clearest understanding, infinitely farther is the distance from the clearest understanding to doing accordingly; indeed, in the first instance there is only a difference of degree, in the other there is an essential difference of kind... — it is my action which changes my life."

Placing one's trust in the power of education to perfect the human condition could only be conclusively refuted as a theory of redemption by man's total destruction. Destroying the world by his own hand loomed as a literal possibility five decades ago at the University of Chicago when Hutchins presided there as Chancellor at the time that the first successful test of atomic fission was made.

More sophisticated methods of destruction have since been devised and of course institutions of higher learning have had a major hand in devising them. The professor is no better guardian of moral values than the representative of any other segment of society. In fact, he is no distinguished guardian even of academic values, as the present condition of the schools, colleges, and universities suggest.

Socrates showed his fidelity to and respect for the nation that educated him by drinking hemlock at its command. But not all educated citizens of Athens would have done the same. As might have been expected, some of them were responsible for his having to drink the hemlock.

History does not show the liberally educated man invariably on the side of truth and righteousness. He can usually be found on either side of a vital issue.

The "habitual vision of greatness" that the Athenians had before them in Socrates — and apart from which, says Whitehead, moral education is impossible — did not keep them from killing him. On the contrary, it was an incitement. The very virtue of his existence — inseparable from his teaching — was an offense to them. ("He hath a daily beauty in his life," says Iago of Cassio, "that makes me ugly.") They had rather that Socrates were dead than teaching them. They understood just enough of one idea that he tried to teach them — namely, that they did not know, as they thought, but only thought that they knew — to suspect that he was being offensive.

The death of Socrates is the most effective refutation of his idea that the good of the state requires a philosopher-king. The philosopher cannot let the wheat of truth and the tares of error grow together, but the wise ruler must.

After being sentenced to death, Socrates magnanimously paid tribute to the State for his education. But, obviously, he and the State had no common understanding of how he should exercise the manhood for which he had presumably been educated. The State that gave him his education to live as a free man took away his life for living as one.

If we look to the State and its system of public education to guarantee our integrity, to whom or to what shall we look to guarantee the integrity of the State? (Who shall guard the guardians?)

A philosopher *qua* philosopher seeks to understand the rational foundations of existence. But how to achieve this understanding is only half the problem of the philosopher-king. No matter how great a philosopher the ruler may be, he is as caught in the moral dilemmas of life — The good that he would, he does not; and the evil that he would not, that he does — as any of his subjects.

To be a philosopher does not necessarily mean to be a certified Great Soul. Even a philosopher can be unloving, unjust, mean-spirited, or evil. Moreover, a "philosopher-king" has not only his own personal problem of how to bring knowledge and practice together in living a good life; but, in addition, the problem of how to use his authority to achieve for his nation the virtue that in his own soul is so deeply in question.

The myth of the philosopher-king as a redeemer of the state is as pervasive in human history — and as misleading — as is the myth of education as social or individual redemption.

The liberally educated man may be expert in drawing up codes of ethics, but this doesn't necessarily mean that there is a close causal connection between his education and any reason for his being trusted further than the man not similarly advantaged.

The presumption that education can guarantee to "produce" a good man or woman is based on a misunderstanding of human motivation. Persons are motivated partly by what they understand the right thing to do and partly despite what they understand the right thing to do.

Education can no more guarantee individual virtue than general suffrage can guarantee good government.

A democratic form of government, in which political authority is based upon the consent of the governed, is more likely to result in a just society than is an autocracy. Understanding, which is an aim of education, is more likely to result in a better individual life than lack of understanding. But, needless to say, these general truths need to be braced by and hedged about with particular and powerful reservations.

We readily condone behavior in ourselves or in our government that we find alarming or repulsive when we discover it in others, no matter how well educated we may be. In 1915 John Erskine, the "father" of the Great Books movement, could write (in *The Moral Obligations To Be Intelligent*): "In history at least, if not yet in the individual, Plato's faith has come true, that sin is but ignorance, and knowledge and virtue are one." But if an intelligent student of the world's history since 1915 did not learn from it that, in history at least, knowledge and virtue are not one, it may be doubted that history could teach him anything worth knowing.

In considering the aims of education, the direct objective should be carefully distinguished from the pervasive hope. Education lacks the power to satisfy all the hopes or quiet all the fears of life. Proficiencies that are observable as the direct result of study and teaching, during and at the conclusion of a course of study, should be the gist of what we mean by educational aims.

The life of excellence that is commonly cited as the aim of liberal education could hardly be objected to as a life goal, although in a pluralistic society there might be some difficulty in reaching general accord on what constitutes its substance; or — depending on what the substance is — on the competence of the schools to do much toward advancing their juvenile charges an appreciable distance in its direction.

The schools are more likely to achieve their aims if they limit them to those within the scope of educational (academic) achievement. Education is a practical art and its mandate should be prescribed by its nature. The aims of education manifest their legitimacy by the reasonable expectation we may have of their attainment. This is true of any practical art. If the right means are used, the ends are practicable. If it were true, that "Education is to make people good, therefore happy," (Mark Van Doren) one could only observe how marvelous is, and has always been, the large gap between its aim and its achievement.

Education, needless to say, can no more guarantee happiness than virtue. Understanding may, in fact, cause more of anger and anguish than happiness, and disturb our peace as often as secure it. Great lives, beautiful for understanding — poets, philosophers, prophets, saints — do not invariably exemplify what we ordinarily mean by happy lives.

These days the schools are not likely to define their objectives in terms of "moral virtue"; instead, economic, psychological, and sociological objectives have taken its place in their philosophies of education.

However, the promise held out by these objectives is as deceptive and mistaken in respect to the appropriate and genuine eduction of Everychild as is the promise that education will make him happy or good.

Where there is no vision of a program that truly educates, no public relations of the School persuasion will succeed in keeping a large number of American children from ignorance, illiteracy, and incompetence as a result of their School experience.

A legitimate educational aim can be recognized by its unmistakable air of subject matter, specificity, and competence. A discipline is stated, a work named, a level of proficiency determined. It has, in short, a substance that suggests limited but significant accomplishment, not the longing for grace and redemption.

Credible educational objectives must be based upon a philosophy that neither downgrades the student's potentialities nor is out of sight of the system's capabilities.

Where the aims of education are realistic — not simply a statement of life's ideals, but attainable by ordinary ability and by a rational and coherent program— their achievement can be reasonably assured.

To learn to use language in its several major forms is to give feeling and thought an extended range; and to learn to interpret language as exemplified in individual works of art is to acquire understanding of the height by which its use is measured. But no matter how well the forms of language are learned, the freedom of using them destructively or deceptively will keep equal pace.

A better world won't be built by ignorance, shallowness, or half-baked ideas. But neither can information, knowledge, or understanding guarantee it. Plain honesty, a healthy sense of humor, and a modest estimate of the self's importance relative to others would probably do more than education can to justify the ways of man.

Education can neither guarantee the purposes for which a life is lived nor predict the effects of its influence upon particular lives. It can exhibit models of possibility, but each individual life responds to its possibilities in different ways.

A good education can hardly guarantee happiness, but it may enrich life and enlarge the horizon of the self and make the society in whose schools education for all is taken seriously a more free, more vital, and more interesting place, in which to live.

In a free, secular, and pluralist society, neither morality, nor metaphysics, nor religion, can furnish the presiding educational principle. The education code does not enact either the *Nichomachean Ethics* or the Ten Commandments. Good books exemplify the power of literary art. The justification for works of literary art in the curriculum must be found not in their power to make for righteousness but in their power to make for literacy.

"The end then of learning," wrote John Milton, for whom religion was the principle by which education should proceed, "is to repair the ruins of our first parents...." The major purpose of early Puritan education was to thwart Satan "that olde deluder." In the California Teachers Association's professional "Code of Ethics," the schools are declared to have as their main objective "development of the whole individual." A lesser creed within the Code states that the teacher prepares the pupil to "be happy personally."

Although it is not the principal function of education to inculcate precepts of moral truth that guarantee happiness or virtue, genuine education exerts a moral influence upon its students in a good teacher, a good book, a good discussion, which are ways of integrity in the context of education, though not readily transferable to other contexts.

But who can say what individual or social value teaching a boy the art of reading will have for him as a man?

If it means that in his teaching the teacher must keep in mind all the major emotional and sociological factors bearing upon the lives of each and every student in his class — indeed, in all his classes — this isn't even funny. If it means that a child is a person, with all human dignities, frailties, and existential crises upon his little head, and that a teacher should have some elementary awareness of what it means to be human, then such understanding had better be taken for granted if anything can.

There is no surer way than School to kill a good thing. There is nothing more therapeutic in the classroom than a teacher who knows how to teach; and the best teachers are likely to be those who interpret their proper function in academic — not psychiatric, moral, metaphysical, religious, political, or sociological — terms.

Who has not known superb teachers who hardly knew the names of their students? Not that the teacher should be indifferent to the individual nature and destiny of his students, insofar as this is humanly possible. Jacques Maritain writes of the most precious gift in an educator "as a sort of sacred and loving attention to the child's mysterious identity, which is a hidden thing that no techniques can reach." But a good teacher will manifest his love and concern by trying to meet the needs that are possible for him to meet. Kindness, warmth, good humor, forbearance, are not incompatible with the disciplines of learning. Neither, however, are they a remedy for economic injustice, racial prejudice, bad housing, unsympathic parents, or acne. Like good architecture, they can go part of the way toward making the classroom a more agreeable place in which to learn.

Albert Jay Nock wrote of the teachers at the college he attended: "If they had once tried to make themselves informal, chummy, big-brotherly — in a word, vulgar — we would have resented it with contempt....There was not a grain of sentimentalism in the institution; on the other hand, the place was permeated by a profound sense of justice...."

Part of the justice due a child is that he not be seduced by the teacher's own sentimental version of the student-teacher relationship. Another part due him is that the height of his learning powers not be prematurely pegged. Nock goes on to say: "The motto of the college might well have been taken from St. Luke's words, 'When ye shall have done all those things which are commanded you, say, We are unprofitable servants.' Yet we rather liked this attitude, as being in a way complimentary."

The main business of the schools should be to teach students how to be good students. The teacher makes his contribution to the education of his students by his competence as a mediator of learning, not as a substitute parent, psychiatrist, sociologist, moralist, or clergyman. The teacher who is a real teacher becomes a way for his students to become real students. What else should they be in the classroom? What else should he?

No educational system will ever be able to respond to the entire, agonizing need of the individual child: to ensure that nothing essential of human worth is lost, strayed, or stolen; that no creative impulse will be frustrated or denied; that what the student seeks, the system will provide; and if he doesn't know what to seek, it will lead him to it, Empathy reigning happily o'er all. What could be more ludicrous than a teachers' college version of divine providence?

Nevertheless, it is true that the educational system must find means of responding to individual need. The system in which the individual person is lost in the shuffle is not educating anyone. Campus demonstrations by college and university students during the Sixties erupted because of various political issues, notably the Vietnam war. But the students were also protesting the factory system of higher learning. A small factory on the elementary school level is no more congenial to the spirit of learning than it is on the higher academic levels.

That the learning process is concerned with an existing, individual student will not be lost sight of by a good teacher or a good educational system. But the best education conceivable is still a long way from the love and attention that every child needs in his personal life.

The justice that is due Everychild in the schools is not so much that he be "understood," but that he be taught understanding. The teacher (or parent) who is more interested in "understanding" him than in getting him to understand will fail miserably at both.

There are various possible selves for a self to be, but not all possibilities are equally desirable. If education cannot help the student understand better whatever it means to be human at its best — or, for that matter, at its worst — then, it might be asked, what essential difference does it make what kind of education he gets? The perennial issues of daily life do not change. It is still a life's work to learn how to live well, and education should have some contribution to make toward solving this problem.

But how can an educational system be held to deliver on this promise? How can the schools and colleges teach anyone to live well if they cannot even teach their students how to learn well? How to live well is a problem for the whole of our lives. How to learn well is a problem for which education purports to be the specific answer. There are few or no experiences of life that cannot be "educational" in some sense — that the honesty, intelligence, stubbornness of man's spirit cannot turn to some constructive use.

If we conceive of education as extending over the entire space of life, meaning all the ways in which we are brought to greater understanding — from reading a great book to experiencing great suffering — then, clearly, we are thinking of it in terms of a meaning that must include the ends of human life. Then reformation, rectitude, and redemption become the last 3 Rs for which the first are taught.

"What is education?" asks Kierkegaard (in *Fear and Trembling*). "I should suppose that education was a curriculum one had to run through in order to catch up with oneself, and he who will not pass through this curriculum is helped very little by the fact that he was born in the most enlightened age."

But "to catch up with oneself" — i.e., *to be*, as distinguished from *to know*, a distinction that Kierkegaard emphasizes throughout his entire work — implies a kind of learning (or education) that concludes only with the end of one's life. In this sense no one is "educated" but only, one supposes, on the way to becoming so.

However, we ought not confuse this meaning of education with the meaning that is concerned with the limited problem of what is possible, desirable, and necessary for schools to be doing. Elementary education can be considered as the first stage in a lifetime of learning; and, as such, to have the ends of life as its ultimate aim. But the aim in this sense would be no different from any other educational institution; or indeed from all other social institutions.

The reach of the schools should exceed their grasp, but not be out of sight. Whatever aims are not achievable in reasonable measure within the time allotted to the curriculum are not aims for which those administering the program can be held accountable.

Undoubtedly, education is concerned with, related to, aspires toward, life and liberty and the pursuit of property.

But also undoubtedly, we must not succumb to the temptation of identifying the practicable objectives that education can reach in a given time available with those that it cannot.

Those aims that are bound up with the ends of human life must be distinguished from those that the schools can and should be commissioned to achieve.

We cannot hold teachers, principals, superintendents of schools, or school boards, responsible for making Everychild happy, moral, or mature. But we can and should hold them responsible for teaching him the languages of learning. This educational aim is not only attainable, but the schools should be held accountable for their attainment.

What each person makes of the abilities and understanding that education can give him is resolved in the total drama of his life. The liberal arts can be, and no doubt often are, employed as means to advance the most useless, not to say malevolent, of ends. When education functions simply as a mirror of society, it lacks the authority to teach students what they ought to know: when it aims to function as a kind of social ideal, it lacks the enabling power to achieve its purpose.

It is within the bounds of reason that Everychild can learn fundamental skills and understand notable examples of the liberal arts. In doing this much — and it is much — education might also on occasion be able to strengthen and clarify in him the vision of a good life and a good society. Most young persons are receptive to this kind of vision.

However, the way to introduce him to criteria of excellence and a vision of greatness is not to be found in the cardboard language of the School textbook, but in the quality of language that is native to education at its best. Moreover, we must distinguish the aims of education in its limited, academic sense from those that extend to the entire life of the individual.

A child with ordinary intelligence can be taught to read. This is irrefutable. If he can be taught to read reasonably well, he can be given an elementary liberal education. This is plausible. But that he will, because of his formal education, thereby and henceforth live the good life is, to say the least, questionable.

Education is no panacea for curing the ills of mankind. Rather, it functions to make more effective whatever the purposes for which we use it.

Education assumes that man is not born to be little in stature, that there is no advantage to burying our talents, that Lilliput is all right to visit but only those of incorrigibly diminutive stature would want to go native there. Education cannot credibly claim to make anyone good, true, or beautiful, but it can provide a better understanding of these indisputably desirable ends. We treasure the great tragedies of dramatic literature because they remind us of the height and depth of our existence.

Education can enlarge the powers of man and broaden his horizon, but it can't change his nature. A Congolese savage is surely no worse — and much less dangerous — than the Nazi with a Heidelberg degree. But the case of the educated Nazi is too obvious. It is not ignorant savages who are to be found at the centers of power in this world.

The theory that education is a dynamic form of existential alchemy, guaranteed to make or keep the self virtuous — needs more proof. One spoils a life — his own or another's — with the best education in the world: his intellect might even help him do it more effectively.

This is not to deny that "life" and "learning" are closely related. Emotional problems affect the ability to learn to read and the failure to learn to read may cause emotional problems. Emotional and intellectual factors (not to mention sociological, biological, moral, political, economic and religious ones) act and react upon each other. But, clearly, there are all too many variables and all too few constants in this interaction.

Man is the only creature in the universe who has both the freedom and the responsibility to become a truer self. But his freedom is his problem. Education cannot guarantee to solve this problem at the same time that it guarantees to enlarge the scope of his freedom.

"One opinion," writes the philosopher Mortimer J. Adler (in the *Great Books of the Western World* essay on "Education") "from which there is hardly a dissenting voice in the great books is that education should aim to make men good as men and as citizens."

The belief that education "can make men good" suggests a view of human nature that is at variance with the very freedom that liberal education is supposed to extend. Even if education could "guarantee" to produce goodness, it might be just as well not to advertise the fact. The temptation to pride inherent in this belief has often proved difficult to resist. This aim of education has always been easily translated into the implicit (and sometimes explicit) claim of the educationally privileged, that they are morally superior because they are educated. The belief subverts itself. It turns a possible righteousness into an impossible self-righteousness.

"Human evil," wrote Reinhold Niebuhr...." is a corruption of its essential freedom and grows with its freedom. Therefore, every effort to equate evil purely with the ignorance of the mind and with the body is confusing and erroneous."

Although education can achieve no higher rung than the righteousness of the scribes, we should pray (outside the classroom) that the schools never get their teeth into the cause of a righteousness more elevated. The temptation to insinuate various "values" into the learning process, other than those inherent in genuine learning itself, is one that the educator must resist. The role of Pygmalion may be tempting but he must put it behind him.

A good teacher will try to help the student use and develop his own mind, not try to get the student to conform to his. The teacher must assume that most of what he "knows" that is of any consequence is, in the last analysis, a matter of opinion — good opinion, it is to be hoped, but opinion, nevertheless. Assuming this, he will be less tempted to induce his students to go and think likewise.

Ideology insinuates itself as it can. Every educational system reveals some ideological taint. Man's spirit has universal inclination, but particular loyalties and affections. However, where individual works of art comprise the program and are selected for reading and discussion, not because they express a particular point of view but, because, whatever their point of view, they express it superlatively, ideology is reduced to a minimum.

The diversity of viewpoints is the best proof that genuine education has no axe to grind other than "to delight the spirit, to enliven the imagination, to refine and clarify discourse and to bring to the whole mind a fuller sense of its inventiveness, singularity, and freedom." (Henry D. Aiken)

In the study of language and of its arts and works of art, the occasion exists for the teacher himself to become an artist and education itself to become a work of art.

It is no failure of nerve, lack of vision, or abdication of responsibility to confess the plain truth that we cannot look to the schools and colleges to produce the "mature individual" or the "great-hearted soul." Educational institutions will never be competent to do any better than trifle with these important aims and still be competent to perform their essential and appropriate functions.

There is morality in the courage to reject (or, as the case may be, affirm) received opinion; there is religion in the passionate longing for truth; there is "mental health" wherever wisdom is given its due. But explicit principles of morality, religion, and mental health are not those by which the educational enterprise proceeds.

Writing of the world-wide spread of public education that had occurred by the beginning of the twentieth century, Herbert Muller declares: "For the first time in history, all people in theory, and most in practice, enjoyed the opportunity to become literate. There is no more extraordinary development in the history of freedom." But by the middle of the twentieth century, it had become a wry commonplace that the spread of literacy can and does proceed apace with the spread of political slavery. The political tyrannies of both fascism and communism found it expedient to combine the teaching of literacy with the propaganda of dictatorship.

The aims of education are more likely to be achieved if they are limited to those clearly within its competence. If we were more knowledgeable about what education cannot accomplish, we might know better what it can and should.

As long as our idea of education remains amorphous, it will be perfectly suited to look as if it were a solution to all the ills of the world. "The answer for all our national problems," declared President Lyndon Johnson in a speech at Brown University, "the answer for all the problems of the world, comes down, when you really analyze it, to one single word — education."

Like a Rorschach pattern, education can look like almost anything that it pleases anyone to see in it. "Do you see yonder cloud that's almost in shape of a camel?" — "By th' mass, and 'tis like a camel indeed." — "Methinks it is like a weasel." — "It is back'd like a weasel." — "Or like a whale." — "Very like a whale." Education must not be thought irrelevant because it cannot solve all the major problems of life, nor should it be glorified in the mistaken notion that it can.

Liberal education can contribute to all the ways of being free — political, social, economic, intellectual, moral, spiritual — but it cannot guarantee any condition of freedom to which it is at best only contributory.

Education extends the self's dominion, but one cannot read all the signs of life as he would read a book, look at a painting, listen to music, or make scientific observations. There are signs for which not even the best education conceivable would be a preparation and for which a purely rational response would be inappropriate; where language or the silence of language enters only as it is vulnerable. "The life of dialogue," writes Martin Buber, "is no privilege of intellectual activity like dialectic. It does not begin in the upper story of humanity. It begins no higher than where humanity begins. There are no gifted and ungifted here, only those who give themselves and those who withhold themselves."

By acquiring greater powers of language the self is free to understand and to do more than it could before; but to exercise these powers wisely and well the powers of language alone do not suffice.

The anti-intellectualism that sees academic achievement as an infallible sign of the Devil is the counterpart of the simplistic view that sees it as a remarkable way of lifting humanity up by the bootstraps to the heights of peace and justice, freedom and happiness.

The proper business of the schools and colleges is to be academic: to be centers for the development of intelligence and the nurturing of imagination; to be places where the faculties that inhere in language are taught well; to be institutions of reasoning together about matters of importance. The most radical thing wrong today with our educational institutions is that this is not how they understand themselves.

George Orwell writes of Dickens: "He attacks the current educational system with perfect justice, and yet, after all, he has no remedy to offer except kindlier schoolmasters....He has an infallible moral sense, but...no ideal of work." What the schools and colleges need more than anything else is an ideal of work; i.e., what they should be doing to use students well (by helping them to use their imagination and intelligence well) which is their appropriate objectives.

Because our educational institutions lack a clear principle of how to proceed, because they lack an ideal of work, what's happening in the daily news takes over.

However, it doesn't seem unreasonable that enhancing the student's use of language may also enhance his ability to cope with various problems, if only to raise the level, and to make more stringent the means, with which these problems will be considered.

The educator will surely hope for the best possible moral and social results from the curriculum. But his hopes ought not be confused with his aims. Education doesn't make *all* the difference in life. A little bit of luck or of grace would probably go further than education in achieving many of life's blessings. But it makes a difference.

The child in Grade One has the same educational aim he will have all of his life: to search out the meanings of life as well as he can. We begin the realization of this aim in childhood, but institutions of learning can be held responsible for taking us only part-way.

Elementary liberal education exhibits ways of learning how to proceed in the quest for meaning. A child looks to his elders for the right means, and they ought to be able to do better than look back deadpan. If the schools do not provide Everychild with the necessary criteria and instruction, "the best things," is it likely that he shall, some day, be grateful for *not* having received this kind of education?

If the schools look out for the cultivation of intelligence and imagination, the students, with the help of other agencies, resources, and institutions of society, will look out for the rest of life themselves. Although we cannot know exactly what bearing a sound education has, or might have, upon the ultimate meaning to which the good life is bound, it seems reasonable to suppose that it can and does have bearing on various levels and patterns of meaning short of the ultimate.

> Is there any one who understands human and political virtue?....The truth is that I have no knowledge of the kind....This reputation of mine has come of a certain sort of wisdom which I possess. If you ask me what kind of wisdom, I reply, wisdom such as may perhaps be attained by man, for to that extent I am inclined to believe that I am wise; whereas the persons of whom I was speaking have super-human wisdom, which I may fail to describe, because I have it not myself; and he who says that I have speaks falsely, and is taking away my character. (*Plato, Apology*)

The kind of wisdom that "may perhaps be attained by man" is an appropriate aim of education. But this aim must be realistic; it cannot be "to produce manhood." Socrates left claims of this kind to the Sophists. One would have to be deficient in a sense of tragedy, a sense of history, or a sense of humor, to look to the schools or colleges as guarantors of human goodness.

To become a good human being is a moral and spiritual achievement that lies outside the competence of liberal education. "Covet earnestly the best gifts," wrote St. Paul, "and yet show I unto you a more excellent way." Whether or not the holder of a school diploma or degree ever becomes a loving person, time alone will tell. But if it be an honest diploma or degree, it will verify that the student has in fact, and at least, received the substance of the education that he should have received.

In professing educational aims, educators must ask themselves: What kind of books or other learning materials, what teaching methods, what kind of program, are necessary to entertain a reasonable expectation of realizing them? A pertinent question regarding any realistic educational aim is: Can it be achieved by and during the duration of the curriculum?

The principal aim of genuine elementary education is to teach Everychild the forms of language — literary, mathematical, musical, visual — that his intelligence and imagination need in order to be used extensively and well.

This is a modest aim. But it is worthwhile and it is achievable.

Chapter V
EDUCATION AND MEANING

*What are works of art for? to
educate, to be standards.*

Gerard Manley Hopkins

L iberal education and individual works of art have to do with each
other because meaning is the central concern of each; the most powerful
meaning in the most significant form.

Education depends upon the arts of language for its substance; the arts of
language depend upon education for understanding. Visual art was the only means
that primitive man had in order to pass on in an enduring way what he thought
significant. This original purpose of art remains. It is as true for the modern artist
as for the primitive, for the literary as for the visual artist, that he wants to secure the
best of himself, the enduring part of his thought and imagination. But he also wants
to say something about that of the world that is not himself.

Art and education at their best are both reminders of the fact that it is something
in life — a great deal — not to be let down.

Art manifests the need of the human spirit to seek meaning and the power of the
human spirit to represent it. "Man's essential idea is spirit," said Kierkegaard, "and
we must not permit ourselves to be confused by the fact that he is also able to walk
on two legs."

Language, which is the most characteristic expression of man's spirit, is made
out of whatever he can turn to the use of meaning: time, space, objects in space,
rhythms of time, human faculties, and all other particularities of a real or imagined
world. It occurs in any way that the self can seize upon to express itself.

Spirit is not only the sovereignty of self that gives meaning to language; it is also
the anxiety of self that needs all the meaning it can get to sustain itself in existence.

Man asserts his will by the same scrap of meaning that he seizes to keep from drowning. The straw that he grasps to save himself, he uses for a scepter when the danger passes.

Language enables man to survive existence and to dominate it. Caught in time and space, he takes them both to make his art. Spirit transforms the appearance of things into new reality, that makes a new form of meaning, that generates a new awareness, that creates a new appearance of things.

The signs and symbols of language not only concentrate, abbreviate, represent — and distort — subjective phenomena, but also establish an independent base of their own by enabling us to think in ways not possible before their invention, as, for example, in the history of musical or mathematical notation.

Ideas are frameworks of reference to compose experience and to bring it into clearer focus. An idea is a "reading" of existence — as it appears to be, or as it could imaginatively or rationally be supposed. The ability to read in this sense may be said to epitomize liberal education.

To read is to observe, to interpret, to evaluate. But a poem, a painting, a mathematical theorem, a piece of music, are read differently, after their own kind, and a clear distinction must be made between the kinds of meaning they transmit and, consequently, the kinds of ways they can and should be read.

"In learning a new language," writes Schopenhauer, "a man has, as it were, to mark out in his mind the boundaries of quite new spheres of ideas, with the result that spheres of ideas arise where none were before. Thus he not only learns words, he gains ideas too."

If this is true of different languages within the language of words, how much more true if one understands mathematics, music, and visual art as languages after their own kind, each having its own distinctive ideas; which, in the cases of music and visual art, cannot be expressed at all in another language.

Mathematical signs bear a one to one correspondence to the ideas for which they stand; are precisely translatable; have both arbitrary (conventional) and universal significance.

Poetry functions in a one-to-many correspondence; is rich and variegated in suggestiveness; has a depth and extension of meaning that is never fully exhausted in the exact terms of the expression. A literary artist trusts the language he uses as adequate to its purpose, not only to express the meaning that he intends but also to allow the openness characteristic of the language of human speech. He knows that he cannot anticipate all possible legitimate readings of his book. "It is art," writes Edgar Wind, "only as long as the ambiguity is sustained."

To "clarify" meaning may, on occasion, lessen its value. "The reclining figure," writes Henry Moore, "is a subject which, for me, is unending. I think if I had five lifetimes I wouldn't exhaust the possibilities in this theme. It may be that it also connects the human figures with landscape more easily than a standing figure could, and landscape is one of my great obsessions, besides the human figure. I think it's a way of the two being amalgamated, but what it all means, I don't really know."

If music employs words for its more explicit and denotative values, words "aspire" to music in their more powerful, memorable, and connotative modes, of which poetry is the supreme example.

Music employs a notation that is both denotative, like mathematics, and connotative, like poetry. (Poetry is the music of speech; mathematics the prose of music.) Musical notes symbolize the tones that are the existent things which compose the music's sounding reality and which are heard denotatively and connotatively at once.

Visual art has no "code" that must be "broken" to use or understand it. Techniques of craftsmanship are concerned with the quality with which this language is employed; they are not, so to speak, conditions of employment. Visual forms transmit visual ideas directly; not indirectly, as symbols do.

Each of the major languages of learning is a distinct way of expressing particular aspects of reality, actual and hypothetical. Language is no mere window through which man looks out on reality. Language and reality interact and intermingle with each other. Language is an inextricable and central part of our reality. In language the self maintains itself in existence.

The integrity of language anchors the world of meaning. The statement, This is a work of art, is a declaration that here is language which engages, or ought to engage if rightly understood, that of ourselves which cannot be held cheaply.

Education has to do with art because art is a way of making vital connections. The languages of learning are a wedding of the world as it is and as it may be imagined or conceived. Individual works of art are a fulfillment of the wedding vows.

The absorption of the artist in his work is not difficult to understand. Language is central to the reality of human existence. What could be more absorbing than work that has so much to do with the center of things?

To provide Everychild the opportunity for a true education is to provide him with the means of being exactly where he wants to be, whether he knows it or not: namely, absorbed in what he is doing. What is art if not the "one flesh" of work and play whose substance matters beyond the artist's own interest and pleasure in what he does? The intrinsic excellence of a work of art is a magnet of interest. The quality of the work answers to the mind's need for the best nutrition it can use.

Art seeks to discover and invent forms, enduring forms. The false futurist, the shallow currentist, the stale traditionalist, have more in common than they know. Prophecy, in art as in life, succeeds not by out-guessing the future, or second-guessing the past, but by exploring the depths of the present. An artist — a man — can be no more than equal to his situation.

The genuine artist knows that he must reach beyond the trivial and express more than the inscrutable. He must put himself at the center of whatever meaning he can command if he would not make suffering Hollywood ludicrous and death TV cheap. A work of art posseses the dignity of having a rational base, of being intelligible. Art is a way of overcoming disorder, not creating it; confounding the banal, not adopting it; resurrecting the lifeless, not exhuming it.

In music and visual art "the sensing of things which escape classification" come into their own and must be given their due as faculties of interpretation.

The arts that have intuition and imagination and sensory perception as their norms should either not be brought into the curriculum at all — which would be a mistake — or else the distinctive ways in which they achieve their meaning should be respected, encouraged, and empowered.

The principle of rationality doesn't have the same significance in visual art as in human discourse. But despite the dependence of each of the liberal arts upon different faculties, each has its own kind of intelligibility, which is closely and significantly related to other kinds in the same self.

On the assumption that this is a meaningful world, education can help the seeker search out some of its meaning; but it can't establish this assumption, which is won only by a wager of the self. The question of the meaning of existence is raised, regardless of education, in the anxious depths of every human heart where the magnitude of the wager is exactly the same for every human being.

Martin Buber's "reading" of a tree in *I and Thou* suggests a vivid analogue to the reading of a book that is "the precious life-blood of a master spirit...." (John Milton)

It is that kind of book that is meant here by a "text" in liberal education, or a "great" book. There are only a limited number of ways to refer to a work — literary, visual, musical, scientific, or mathematical — that is generally thought to be among the best of its kind. Buber's reading of a tree might also be thought of as an analogue of liberal education, even as is reading itself at its most extensive and significant levels.

"I consider a tree." writes Buber. "I can look on it as a picture: stiff column in a shock of light, a splash of green shot with the delicate blue and silver of the background."

Obviously, one of the primary ways of considering a tree is as one would look at any visual object. We look at a tree in its sensuous, "literal" being — what is immediately observable if one has the eye and the mind to see what is there to see.

By the same token, reading a text requires us to read it literally, as written; that is, as the words appear immediately to us in the sense that corresponds to the perceptive one in considering a tree.

However, in reading a text we add a new dimension to our understanding of it when, at least at first, we are able to read it sympathetically, informed by the mind and spirit of the writer as he intends his work to be read.

The careful reader will want to know — if only for the sake of his own intellectual integrity — not only what the writer says, literally, but also what he means by what he says: the connotation as well as the denotation of his words. And, even further than that, a great book — not to mention any text of high quality — deserves, as nearly as possible, and at least initially, the kind of sympathetic reading by which alone the reader can ascertain the meaning that resonates in the writer's individual voice.

In the translation of a passage written in a foreign language, we may gain some idea of its meaning even though it considerably distorts the writer's intent. The reader will be reading a much different text from the one written. It happens not infrequently that the reviewer of a book will misrepresent it simply because his prejudices prevent him from considering it — even with good intentions, even for a moment — from the writer's point of view. (The same picture looked at from two entirely difference angles — perhaps one right side up and the other upside down — can hardly be said to be seen as the same picture.)

By no means is this to say that a sympathetic reading need preclude a critical or an unfavorable evaluation of a work. On the contrary, both a literal and a sympathetic reading of a text are an indispensable preliminary to a close interpretation and a fair evaluation of it, favorable or otherwise.

In a reader's immediate impression of a book, he may find it incomprehensible, wrong and wrong-headed; in a word, unreadable. Sometimes even a great novel or a great poem may seem upon the first reading like the thought of someone whose grasp of reality is barely tenable. Nevertheless, the resolute reader may still want to try to discover what this lunatic means by what he says, why he chooses these specific words, this particular mode of expression, and not some other.

What! exclaims the reader. You compare the words of a great poet with those of a lunatic? Well, it has been done. "The lunatic, the lover, and the poet / Are of imagination all compact.... / And as imagination bodies forth, / The forms of things unknown, the poet's pen / Turns them to shapes and gives to airy nothing / A local habitation and a name." (*A Midsummer Night's Dream*)

Although the words of both the lunatic and the poet may be "of imagination all compact, " those of the former would, presumably, be of interest only to himself (and his psychiatrist), but those of the latter — because of their power, beauty, truth — would, presumably, be of universal interest. Is there any civilized country in the world where the writer of the above lines of poetry is not known and revered?

In his further contemplation of a tree, Buber goes on to say of it, "I can perceive it as movement: flowing veins of clinging, pressing pith, suck of the roots, breathing of the leaves, ceaseless commerce with earth and air — and the obscure growth itself."

This description in terms of "movement" can also be seen as corresponding to a metaphor of music — music as an association, an intimation, of whatever in life has motion, including both the growth of a tree and that of a great musical work, each mysterious and wonderful in its own development.

By considering a tree in this way, Buber suggests a more intimate — and therefore more moving — relation. The sensuous elements are given a different form, adding the musical to the visual consideration, an "obscure growth" in our understanding of the tree.

Buber continues: "I can classify it in a species and study it as a type in its structure and mode of life."

Here the description moves away from an apprehension of the tree in its physical aspects to one that is abstract, conceptual, scientific.

Furthermore, writes Buber of the tree, "I can subdue its actual presence so sternly that I regard it only as an expression of law....I can dissipate it and perpetuate it in number, in pure numerical relation."

At this stage of the description, so great is the separation in our considering the tree from its actuality that we can no longer tell where the connection is between the abstraction it has become and the particular living tree we know.

By excluding all sensuous ways of apprehending the individual tree, we "subdue its actual presence." We lose the tree for the concept. The living tree we have been considering becomes a shadowy remembrance, a mere number.

This is not of course to deny that the study of nature should be as "scientific" as possible and that nature in general should be used for the benefit of human nature. But if in so doing we lose sight of the particulars in which nature has its direct, actual presence — a tree, for example — we may be paying too high a price for the benefits; we may, by using nature indiscriminately, indifferently, imprudently, impersonally, discover that these apparent benefits have proved to be more of a problem or a disaster than a boon.

A tree is a not impossible place to begin the study of science in our schools: one of the countless particulars of nature out of which the "laws" of science are derived.

We might do worse in studying science as part of a liberal arts curriculum than to study it not merely in terms of number, classification, type, species, process, structure, and the like, but also as a meeting place of scientific abstractions, on the one hand, and the local habitations of human life, on the other.

A mere narrow, technological, vocational, approach to the study of nature must not only prove wearisome to the soul of the ordinary student but greatly diminish his comprehension and appreciation of nature and of mankind's responsibility for and relation to it.

As in the contemplation of a tree, there are various modes of which a work of art, literary or otherwise, may be interpreted. The greater the work the more likely it will lend itself to various interpretations. Needless to say, these will not all be equally valid, useful, or interesting.

Like a tree, a text becomes more problematic as we move further away from considering it in literal terms and move toward considering it in interpretive terms.

Buber's concluding step in his description of possible ways to consider a tree is different in kind from all the other ways.

He writes: "It can, however, also come about, if I have both will and grace, that in considering the tree I become bound up in relation to it....To effect this it is not necessary for me to give up any of the ways in which I consider the tree. There is nothing from which I would have to turn my eyes away in order to see, and no knowledge that I would have to forget. Rather is everything, picture and movement, species and type, law and number, invisibly united in this event.

"Everything belonging to the tree is in this: its form and structure, its colours and chemical composition, its intercourse with the elements and with the stars, are all present in a single whole."*

This description is clearly not just how one may look at a tree but how one may look at a world: how one may compose the elements of a world to achieve, or try to achieve, a unity and harmony among them.

And it is not just how we may look at a world but by implication how we may observe, interpret, and express ourselves and our relation to it in all the ways at our command: in words and in facial expression, in tones of voice and in gesture, in the ways we dress, spend money, use time, manage place, and however else we communicate our points of view, what we believe and who we are. But the primary and most telling of these is the language of words.

It is in the language of human speech and in the silences of speech, in thought and in the chaos of thought, that we are most closely "bound up in relation" to the world or to any part of it. It is in this language that we are best enabled to navigate upon the sea of meaning. And if our educational objective is liberal in nature, where else should we look for "navigators" if not to those masters who have so powerfully expressed the genius of human discourse?

Precisely because the writings of these masters do not speak to us with one

*This and preceding quotations from *I and Thou* are taken from Ronald Gregor Smith's translation, 2nd ed. New York, Charles Scribner's Sons, 1958.

accord as to the course we should set upon our voyage of seeking true worth; but only by virtue of these writings — which in some instances have been a central part of cultural history for millennia — as paradigms of language, that liberal education looks to them for criteria of teaching and learning.

The responsibility is ours, individually and collectively — as in a democracy it must be — to set ourselves the course that we would take. Our navigators by and large can only establish in the quality and power of their thought how we might best proceed.

This is not, for example, to suggest that reading scientific works is the only or the best way to study nature. But we are here concerned with the reading of a text as an analogue to the "reading" of nature that we do in the laboratory and in the field (earth, water, sky), both of which are essential to the study of scientific subjects on any level of learning (and by extension as an analogue also to the other liberal arts).

In discussing a text in class, the question is not, Which interpretation is the "right" one? but, rather, on the basis of the literal text and the discussion about it, Which are the better or best interpretations?

Clearly, this latter question is one that must be decided by each participant for himself upon the basis of whatever interpretations appear to him to be the most valid in the light of the conceptual and imaginative truth he sees in them; and he will decide this by whatever critical faculties — knowledge, wisdom, imagination, maturity, experience (or their lack) — he is able to bring to bear upon the questions. (And despite the obvious limitations of youth, a youngster may bring an insight to a work of literature that would escape the apprehension of an older person).

In the class discussion of a text, in school or college, each participant is obliged to test his opinions against those of others. A critical reading will take place best when the reader's ideas are challenged in discussion and he is obliged to defend them. Otherwise, he is in danger of confining himself to his own intellectual ghetto, a condition not unknown in the academic, departmentalized world of Higher Learning.

We make a personal judgment of a text not simply in terms of whether we like it or not, agree with it or not, according to our own and to common experience. But we also distinguish, deliberately or not, between those books whose intellectual and imaginative qualities may be first-rate beyond dispute; and those works, great or not, which affect our lives profoundly, and regarding which we might think upon finishing one, I'm not the same person I was before I read this book.

Very few books in the course of a lifetime of reading are likely to fall into this latter category, possibly even only one. A book of this kind is crucial insofar as it lights the way for us to compose our experience of the world we live in. (And of course something less than a profound effect may also make the reading of a particular book memorable in our lives.)

A book that is crucial to us enables us to know what it means to be, in Buber's words, "bound up in relation" to it (and, vicariously, to its author). By radically changing our outlook, our way of considering the world, it becomes different in kind from the many other books we may have read. It becomes a kind of sacred object. Its merit or lack of merit as an intellectual work may be fully recognized ("There is nothing from which I would have to turn my eyes away in order to see, and no knowledge that I would have to forget.") but these considerations become incidental to the change in us that it has effected.

Liberal education, like a tree, is rooted in the soil of language, branches out in every direction, is nurtured by the dew of imagination and the sun of intelligence, is not merely the sum of its parts but is present in a single whole. Everything connects.

Chapter VI

THE LANGUAGE OF WORDS: THE PRIMARY LANGUAGE

> If they {everyday words} suddenly began to function in the fullness of their true meanings, if upon our pronouncing and hearing them our minds understood at once their essential meanings, we would be frightened in the presence of the basic dramas which they contain.
>
> Ortega Y. Gasset

I t is as impossible to conceive of human beings with the power of true speech but no spoken language with which to communicate as it is to conceive of a language that was, so to say, there before human beings existed to speak it. Whether or not man "invented" human speech is the other side of the question of his own creation.

Originally, a word was a dream, and its most powerful use invariably retains something of a dream-like quality: that is, the power to astonish, illuminate, rejoice, put in fear; clear yet mysterious.

The language of words is representative of the mind at large, capable of being expressed as precisely as mathematics, as suggestively as music. It is the vehicle of science and of poetry, of collective and of individual sensibility.

In ordinary speech when we say "language" we mean the language of words. The power given Adam to name the animals placed him in a real world, not a world of shadows. ("And whatsoever Adam called every living creature, that was the name thereof.") The power of speech is the breath by which man becomes — or betrays — himself.

Studying the language of speech is, in part, a learning of its structure and best usage; and, in part, a discovery of its awesome nature.

This language comprises both literary tradition and the organic life of the community. In the language of words there are expressed the separate arts and literatures of poetry, history, science, politics, drama. In it there are also reflected the chronicle and values, the everyday needs and wants, the trivia and quandaries, of human life. Languages are levers by which man moves his world; but the language of words is the particular and primary analogue of the world in which as man he lives.

Genuine education guards, strengthens, and transmits the integrity of language.

But the lines of communication down, the lonely individual results in the lonely crowd, and the lonely crowd explodes into the raging mob.

In the Tower of Babel all are prisoners. Words embarrass, estrange, divide us from each other and each from himself. Those who love each other twist the simple meaning of a word to twist each other's heart.

Evil communications not only corrupt good manners but sanity also. The most significant symptom of derangement is the dissociation of speech and reality. The violent as a grammar of irony, confusion as a rhetoric of resentment, the banal as a logic of frustration — are language against itself; the speech of despairing minds.

The truly formless, unintelligible, insane, cannot be "understood"; their sole "purpose," the mystery of their "meaning," is against itself, against understanding. Unhappy ghosts haunt our speech — "What do you mean? Who are you?"

It is a commonplace of linguistic studies that the structure and diction of a language control, limit, and generate the thought that is possible in it (the "Whorfian hypothesis"). The language in which a problem, issue, experience, or relation is expressed establishes the ways of thinking about it. In seeking a true word, we seek a true self. All intellectual and spiritual odysseys are in search of a lost speech in which the self may once again know and be known. Kierkegaard conceived it as his work in life to explain to those who call themselves Christians what the words of Christian faith mean.

We think of the language of words as one in which thought naturally precedes its expression. However, the immediacy of speech suggests a profounder and subtler mutuality between words and thought. Language generates thought not only in its structures but also in its pre-structural and trans-structural presence. The drama of existence is enacted in the words we choose and those that we are given to choose. Words have their roots both in the world of spirit and of time. In the progression of time, the thought precedes the word; but in the eternity of spirit, the Word is the beginning.

Nothing in the current practices of American pedagogy has enraged parents more than The Great American Reading Problem. They see this as an educational crime and they see their children as its helpless victims.

School authorities, on the other hand, are inclined to throw this problem right back into the parents' laps and blame the home environment. As one School director of guidance and counseling defined the Problem: "The chief cause, as we all know, is due to emotional disturbances at home." Parental protests about the dismal reading achievement of their children are seen as contumacious of School authority and threatening to Schoolbook publishers' profits. But it is not improbable that there is a causal relation between the quality of books used in the schools and the quality of reading taught there.

The appropriate books for an elementary liberal education are those that are the best that children can learn to read. They will never learn anything more valuable in their educational life than the rudiments of reading — but they will never learn to read well with inferior books.

Learning to read is a paradigm of the educational process. Learning to read good books is a logical extension of reading's generative power.

There is an ominously voluminous literature of the rudiments of reading instruction. One work cites over a hundred "causes" of reading difficulty, the most thought-provoking of which is "undescended testicles."

In "Let's Be Practical About Reading," an article in *American Education* (published by the then U. S. Office of Education), the use of an elaborate medical terminology — e.g., "early diagnosis and treatment," "reading clinics," "reading disabilities," "corrective techniques," "remedial help," "seriously disabled readers," "intensive diagnosis," "prescriptive teachings" — suggests that the mere fact of a child learning to read puts him, at best, among the walking wounded and, at worst, among the victims of plague.

It declares, in words that speak for virtually the entire corps of "reading experts": "No one method works for all children."

"The reading teacher," it goes on to say, "uses a variety of techniques to stimulate language and learning." For example, "he might use a rock collection or a trip to the natural history museum to build vocabulary and other reading skills." Additional "techniques" recommended are: "puppets, toys, and language development materials." No mention here of good books.

This dictum from the castle keep of American education predictably concludes that "definitive research on specific aspects of how individuals learn to read must yet be done." And of course more money to conduct the research.

The fundamental cause of the Reading Problem cannot be blamed on the stupidity of the American school student, who is as intelligent as students elsewhere; it must be blamed on the methods used to teach him.

Problems tend to become insoluble in proportion to the inappropriateness of the means employed to solve them.

"Anyone who has kept tabs on the deterioration of America's public educational system," writes Samuel L. Blumenfeld "knows that the reading problem is at the heart of it, simply because you can't learn much unless you can read with some proficiency."

Education is unashamedly centered in the book. "Democratic society is a daughter of books," wrote Ortega y Gasset, "the triumph of the book written by man...over the book of laws dictated by the autocracy." By learning how to read a book well a student learns something of the ways to distinguish sober from snap judgment; he learns to look for the pertinent evidence and to find the jugular issue; he learns that an iron opinion or a strong feeling is not a proof.

That reading (reading!) should so tax the competence of the schools that teaching it well proves difficult or impossible is a not insignificant sign of the intellectual abyss into which they have fallen.

The rudiments (or "mechanics") of reading should be taught by a method that assumes a fundamental relation between the way that words sound and the way that they are spelled; in other words, a phonetic method.*

"The operations of writing and reading must seem," writes Edward Gibbon in his *Autobiography*, "on an abstract view, to require the labor of genius — to transform articulate sounds into visible signs by the swift and almost spontaneous motion of the hand, to render visible signs into articulate sounds by the voluntary and rapid utterance of the voice. Yet experience has proved that these operations of such apparent difficulty, when they are taught to all may be learned by all, and that the meanest capacity in the most tender age is not inadequate to the task."

School administrators can relate numerous "reasons" why an apparently intelligent child in the sixth grade is reading at a third grade level. (These levels are themselves wholly inadequate, but that's another issue.) However, no School potentate is likely to be heard to say that the methods used or the system itself is in any way at fault. The teachers are "educated," "dedicated," and "experienced"; the "basal" readers have been "produced" by a blue-ribbon committee of reading experts; and the school has a Remedial Reading Clinic for those students whose "negative family factors" may be showing.

The reasons given by School officials may appear mysterious and unconvincing to the uninitiated; but the unhappy results of School incompetence in this crucial matter of reading instruction have become increasingly manifest to all, except confirmed School apologists.

If a student is to develop an expectation of pleasure and profit from reading, his experience in the classroom must help accustom him to it. The books must be good and the discussion about them must be lively and competently led.

There is, unfortunately, nothing about a School textbook or a typical Schoolroom discussion to encourage these expectations. The schools neglect the best reading machine ever invented. A good book is the secret weapon of education. It has not been, nor is it likely to be, rendered obsolete by any computer or other School hardware presently in sight.

Teaching students how to read and to discuss a good book is the heart of education. What could be more of a truism — or a truth that the schools more unaccountably slight?

Let's Read: A Linguistic Approach, by Leonard Bloomfield, and Clarence L. Barnhart (Detroit: Wayne State University, 1961) is an authoritative work that teaches reading by this method.
How To Read A Book, by Mortimer J. Adler (New York: Simon and Schuster, 1940) proposes a rigorous method of reading that relates its art to that of liberal education.

It may be that the schools do not rightly see how to decide upon the first-rate. The notion may seem presumptuous. It may suggest some kind of undemocratic hierarchy. But it is difficult to see how this ordering by rank is to be avoided in the educational process. A selection of some kind must be made. The quality of what students learn to read appears a not implausible gauge of the quality of their education. Trying to teach students to read well apart from the influence and example of the ranking members of this hierarchy is not only disrespectful but impracticable.

The judgment as to which literary works are most appropriate for study at each level of learning must be open to continual question. One can only confront present responsibility with present wisdom. There is no fixed canon, although it seems reasonable to suppose that certain literary achievements have, as it were, substantial tenure; and that certain works are more suitable for study at one level of intellectual maturity than at another.

The most searching questions can find their occasion anywhere, in any event, at any time. But learning at its best requires something better than fifth-rate textbooks to provide the occasion.

Moreover, when the content of the work is inferior, it cannot be taken up in a way that is decisive. Since learning to give close attention to what is important is a primary aim of education, students must be provided works of study that have the power to compel, as well as the merit to deserve, such attention. More often than not, the occasion of genuine learning will be provided principally by the intrinsic value of what is to be learned — whether a poem, essay, piece of music, mathematical idea, painting or sculpture. The intellectual and artistic value of the work is not incidental to its educational value.

A frozen list of classics can be as deadly to the spirit of genuine education as any other doctrinaire approach. But keeping this caution well in mind, where else should the schools look for the source and substance of intellectual and imaginative power if not to individual works of art?

Adults can learn something from fifth-rate work — with the aid of irony. But children are deficient in this quality. Irony is a privilege of distance, of transcendence, of maturity. No transcendence, no irony. We cannot in good conscience give a child the fifth-rate and leave it to his irony to transcend it.

But are typical School textbooks fifth-rate? Perhaps they are seventh or eighth-rate. It becomes too nice a point. There is a difference in quality between the Schoolbook and an individual work of literary art that requires each to be considered on a different kind of scale from the other. If the best of children's literature is first-rate, where would that leave Dick and Jane, or their current successors? Ninety-eighth-rate? One hundred and sixty-fourth-rate? In comparison with works of literary genius, Schoolbooks are non-ratable. School teachers who gladly teach with the non-ratable are non-teachers who produce non-students.

The quality of the book that a teacher is competent to teach is a measure of his skill. But a Schoolbook has too little power to measure this competence., "The beautiful bare text for me," writes Robert Frost in one of his letters. "Teachers who don't know what to do with it, let them perish and lose their jobs." Even a great book can be ruined for a class by a poor teacher; as even a superb teacher, forced to use Schoolbooks, cannot teach much above them.

If a good or great book is the criterion by which other books are measured, by what criterion are Schoolbooks measured? In School they are measured by School criteria. "But they measuring themselves by themselves, and comparing themselves among themselves, are not wise." That a writer's greatness is recognizable by the artistry with which he handles important themes is one-half of literary culture's notorious leap into circularity; the other half is that we are more able to recognize that a theme is important when a great writer has opened our eyes to its importance.

One generation's elegance may be another's museum piece. A work once thought great may have become merely a relic. "Some of the ancient poets," wrote Frost, "whose names are known and there's nothing to show for it....The poems had no value, but it looks as if they had because they survived....Some things survive by just luck...So time isn't a sure judge any more than anything else is."

There is no sure judge — yet the judgment must be made. The criterion by which we make our judgment must be the same that we apply to any work, ancient or modern. Education shouldn't have to waste its reverence upon works that may once have spoken to the condition of a living generation but do so no longer.

In selecting appropriate materials for a genuine education, the educator must walk a tightrope between works that may have an immediate impact but clearly no lasting value and those whose reputations have endured beyond their deserving.

Most books that survive the passage of time do so by more than just luck. "They [great books] exist," wrote Lionel Trilling, "in the lively milieu that is created by the responses that have long been given to them. For centuries they have been loved and admired and considered and interpreted and quarrelled over — and used, *used*. [his emphasis] Some part of their reality consists in the way they have figured in the life of the world, certainly in the intellectual life of the world, a large part of which is constituted by what has been said about them."

It is incredible that the schools are so indifferent to the questions: Which are the good and great books? When should they be introduced into the curriculum? How should they be discussed? But it is not incredible that, being indifferent to these questions, they fail.

The close relation between learning the language of words and the quality of the books studied is illustrated by the teaching method of the eighteenth-century philosopher Johann Georg Hamann, to whom, a study of his contribution to language theory declares, "Language instruction was the occasion for immediate encounter with the best a language has to offer; hence, it was but natural that Shakespeare was regarded as the gateway to English." He tutored Herder in English by beginning with *Hamlet*.

This is not to suggest a literal imitation of his method in teaching school children. But it may be a good idea to begin their reading and continue it according to Hamann's principle, as it might be applied at each step along the way.

C. S. Lewis, speaking of university education, remarks that: "The simplest student will be able to understand a very great deal of what Plato said; but hardly anyone can understand some modern books on Platonism. It has always therefore been one of my main endeavors as a teacher to persuade the young that first-hand knowledge is not only more worth acquiring than second-hand knowledge, but is usually much easier and more delightful to acquire."

The value of a book can be measured, at least in part, by the meaning — the widened horizon, the deeper understanding — we gain in reading it. This accession of power depends not only upon the quality of the book but also upon the quality of our reading of it. The better the book, the better the reading it deserves; the better the reading, the shorter the distance between the author and the reader whom he addresses.

Needless to say, not all reading for Everychild will be or need be on this level of seriousness. There is of course a place for recreational reading also. But, in fact, as every habitual reader knows, there is no necessary conflict between "serious" reading and reading for pleasure. It's only the kill-joy School philosophy that insists upon Hard or Easy as the crucial distinction to be made between books. The best books, as a general rule, give the most satisfaction— if read with the attention they deserve — because they address much more of the person than do the easy entertainments. A proper education would have its priorities on straight. If Fun is the only name of the game, Education won't be.

When the value of reading good books is not adequately appreciated — then of course School will deserve the opprobrium that has overtaken it, then of course it will fail to educate, then of course it will lose public confidence and esteem.

A good education would teach reflective reading. (Speed reading is for executives.) Reform of reading in the schools might do worse than begin by adopting the principle that only books which deserve to be read more than once should be read even once.

"No book is really worth reading at the age of ten," writes C. S. Lewis, "which is not equally (and often far more) worth reading at the age of fifty....The only imaginative works we ought to grow out of are those which it would have been better not to have read at all." How many School textbooks would pass this test?

A course of study that is good enough to be enjoyed for itself is the kind of education that anyone would want if he could get it. It is not incredible that a school student might want to read a good book for the pleasure of its company. A student with a particular interest in any part of the curriculum should be put in the way of good things in it, to indulge himself to his heart's content.

If all that a teacher sees for his students in reading a work of literary art is that the better it is, the "harder" it is — and the more promising an occasion to convert it into an exercise at hard or trivial labor — he is obviously a stranger to the pleasure of reading, and therefore unqualified to teach it.

If good paperbacks were used extensively in the schools, and students owned the books required by the curriculum, they would be able to underline, write in and therefore study more closely, what they were reading. This would also give them a start in building a good collection of their own. Physical possession of books might be one of the preliminaries to their intellectual possession.

According to School experts, children should read only the books that they have already proved, by reading other books with a similarly limited vocabulary, that they can "cover." This poses the question, How can children get past that first good book, which is sure to be at least partly over their heads? Given the "reading readiness" assumption, this question presents a formidable hurdle. It is a question that logically suggests the next one, How can children ever learn to read well? (How can Achilles ever catch up to the Tortoise?)

A six-year-old of normal intelligence is ready to learn to read. This readiness doesn't need to be taught, but must be assumed (unless proved otherwise) as having already been developed in the normal growth of his intelligence. If the readiness to learn to read had to be taught, then perhaps readiness of readiness would have to be taught also — and so on.

An appropriate degree of maturity is needed to pursue certain subjects and read certain books. "Things growing are not ripe until their season." But in the meantime, there are the studies and books for which the time is now. Each stage of development has its own degree of ripeness. There is never a time in the curriculum that is not ripe for the study of the first-rate that is appropriate at that time.

The acute, chronic, and endemic School fear of teaching above the student's head inhibits the teacher's use of his own intelligence and frustrates the student's need to reach beyond his intellectual grasp. The readability of a book is, to say the least, different from what the experts understand as the readiness of a child to read it. "Aside from the fact," writes a childrens' librarian of Beatrix Potter, "that she was not afraid to use quite long words for the very young, if they were just the right words, there is neither prettiness, preciousness, nor sentimentality in her pages. There is even in her books what is quite astonishing when you consider the youth of her readers, a kind of faint irony of expression, a wonderful pithiness, dryness, toughness."

With the right words the world becomes, for children as well as for adults, at once new and yet more familiar. If we did not already have some understanding of the world that the writer depicts for us, he could not make it more understandable.

But if he succeeded only in placing it in the same light by which we already know it, he would fail to remind us of the world's — and of the word's — power to be astonishingly and everlastingly new.

Schoolbooks fail so dismally to interest Everychild in reading because they are too familiar — hence, stale; because they remind him of nothing important of which he needs reminding — hence, trite; because they use a castrated diction — hence, sterile. In the circumstances, it should be no great test of ingenuity to discern why the schools do not succeed in teaching school students to read well or to enjoy good books.

School seems to be much more intimidated by the possibility that a child will see a word in print that he does not know than to be interested in the possibility of teaching it to him. So why start him down this scary path of real books where he is likely to encounter unfamiliar words?

What can be read at all can be read accurately. Here is a point of seriousness at which education might begin. Learning to read accurately is the modest but indispensable beginning of elementary education.

The elementary school pupil should learn to respect all the particularities of language. Good pronunciation, legible handwriting, correct spelling, exact diction, may be social assets in some circles, liabilities in others. But regardless of class or caste use, they increase an understanding of language and help conduct meaning to its destination.

The School reading experts cannot be accused of being indifferent to emotional factors (however curiously they interpret them), but they are inexplicably careless of intellectual ones. "The effects of a reading program based upon a restricted vocabulary and simplified texts," writes Selma Fraiberg, a national authority on the psychology of children, "reach into all other parts of the curriculum in the elementary grades. The average child in the fourth grade with a reading vocabulary of 1,500 words must be provided with texts in history, geography, and physical science that do not tax his limited vocabulary and shaky mechanical skills. This means, of course, that the texts are severely restricted in content and that the diction is in a class with that of Dick and Jane....

"The effects of this downgrading are seen most clearly in the teaching of literature. As we have already noted, the problems of achieving simple mechanical skill in reading occupy a major part of the curriculum during the first six grades. The average child who has completed the typical fifth-grade reader has a reading vocabulary in the range of 2,500 words. He has been cut off from the best of children's literature and provided with a kind of subliterary sludge...."

Everychild needs a book done by a writer, not a committee. He needs a book he will love to read, not a "learning tool"; not a warmed-over Schoolbook whiff of what someone, somewhere, might once have thought or felt. How can we interest him, how can we *educate* him, this way?

Children are as responsive to what is alive, as interested in the genuine and as disaffected by the phony, as their elders. Cheap, attention-getting tricks may succeed in capturing a transient interest. But it's a losing battle. The law of diminishing returns asserts itself. Where can you go but down — from cheap science to fake technology, from dinosaurs to *Your Telephone and How It Works*. At some point in this process of ersatz learning, the little scholars are no longer with it. Interest is gone. Only their indentured bodies and the mere appearance of attention — just enough to avoid it — remain.

The way to teach a child the language of words — in reading, in writing, in speaking, in listening — is to teach him with examples of its power and glory.

To say the least, this is not a novel precept. Neither, by any stretch of the imagination, can it be said to be a practiced one in the schools today. "The contemporary scene," wrote Mark Van Doren in 1943, "is filled with educators who want to protect students from the classics: which they do not burn but which they would keep on the back shelves. Their compassion, almost tearful at moments, is for a generation of youth threatened with direct exposure to the best spirits that have lived. Such an exposure, they say, imperils health and sanity in the tender and growing mind."

If there were a single justification for the invidious distinction that came to be made in this country during the 1940s and 1950s between "educators" and "educationists," it would be that the former do not, characteristically, fear the influence of good books on children; but that the latter, characteristically, do. Educationists do not burn the great and good books; they substitute watered-down, homogenized, committee-written, non-books for them. These are manufactured strictly for School use. A child would have to be incorrigible to be educated by them.

A school that understood the real nature of education would consider that it had hardly any higher aim than that of making good books of substantial interest to its students. It would consider school years a good time and school a fine place for students to learn to read well and to acquire a taste for the pleasure and value of reading.

That good books are necessary to teach children how to read well, that this is in fact the most important part of education, and that the schools fail miserably in this vital area of their responsibility — all this is old hat. But only the School establishment ever appears to wonder, Why all the continued fuss about it?

It came as a tremendous revelation in the forties, that infants need physical affection, Tender Loving Care. Infants need affection! What a discovery — or rediscovery — at this stage of human history! Obviously, there is a mint to be mined in the obvious. That good teachers using good books are a potent educational combination can hardly lay claim to being an original notion. But in present educational circumstances, it can make a fair claim to the necessity of being rediscovered.

The wholesale burning of books is barbarous. But the burning of Schoolbooks — or at least their elimination from the schools — could be inspiring. Good books would be held in greater esteem. Children would learn that what looks like a book may be only a Schoolbook. It would be an object lesson in the distinction to be made between appearance and reality. Education would be on its way.

Schoolbooks enter the learning experience of Everychild only to cheapen and dull it. They put the School blight on learning before it has fairly begun.

On the one hand, there is the world of Schoolbooks; and, on the other, there is the world of real art, real thought, real imagination, which are the substance of a real education. Two distinct cultures: School *versus* Education.

An article on the schools describes the writing in Schoolbooks as "cereal box prose" and provides an example: "Columbus came to the New World in 1492. It took a long time to get here. The land he saw later was called America. Now it is the greatest country in the world." This, in the fifth year of Schooling.

"By a *textbook*, as opposed to a *text*," writes Eva Brann, "I mean manuals of...teaching material written in conventional technical language. Textbooks, then, are opposed to works that are original in both senses of the term, in being the discoveries or reflection of the writer himself, and in taking a study to its intellectual origins....

"And this innocuous-seeming enterprise textbook-making turned out to be the most insidiously potent of all the repudiations of the textual tradition...."

Real art sharpens and brightens the edge of existence; it dramatizes the possibility of making time pay dearly, so that when death comes, it is no mean loss. A work of liberal art is language that governs; it is a criterion. Insofar as education is remote from the sovereign centers of learning, it is Schooling, not Education.

Every serious reading of a work of art is, at once, a study of its individual meaning and worth; a study of the art it expresses; a study of the language in which it is expressed; and a study of the "reality," existential or conceptual, with which it connects.

The destiny of a work of art is to endure; the fate of a Schoolbook is to become obsolete. As a consequence, there are in the main two fundamentally different, fundamentally opposed, kinds of "education," each based upon the kind of learning material that is most characteristic of it. Works of literary art relate the student to the real world, as Schoolbooks do not; they satisfy a thirst for the genuine, as School-books cannot.

School has devised its own materials of study and its own standards of judgment in respect to them. The student who knows only this culture is excluded from the reality of which genuine art is the expression. A Schoolbook is no valid entry into a real world.

Youngsters are dependent upon the integrity and competence of their teachers and elders to introduce them to criteria that deserve to be taken seriously. Students have the right to expect, from the First Grade, that they shall be initiated into a world of validity; and that they will not have to waste the school years of their lives getting ready for the genuine article.

The schools have criteria, methods, materials all their own. This is the secret of their failure. They are a bridge to nowhere. As an educational institution, School has no vital signs; it is an intellectual ghost.

If Schoolbooks are written only for School, for whom are works of literary art written? Well, who can tell exactly for whom, or why, they are written? Kierkegaard wrote his books for his "single reader." The usual motive for writing a Schoolbook is a publisher's contract. But a serious writer has a story to tell, an idea to explore. His work is original. He has no pre-fabricated, pre-packaged "units" to sell. He is a person, on a voyage of discovery; he is a single human being, not a committee. He may think well or poorly of his book; have written it in jest, desperation, hunger, or pain. However, motive aside, we are obliged to take his work seriously if it exemplifies the beauty and power of genuine speech.

In Walter Kaufmann's Prologue to Buber's *I and Thou*, he writes: "Among the most important things that one can learn from Buber is how to read.... We must learn to feel addressed by a book, by the human being behind it, as if a person spoke directly to us. A good book or essay or poem...is the voice of You speaking to me, requiring a response."

We should no more allow cheap-jack Schoolbooks to be used in the education of Everychild than we would allow a moron as his classroom teacher.

What is meant here by "reading" a literary work as liberal education uses the term is, in Eva Brann's words, "all the ways of paying attention to texts, from mere etymology to an account of the meaning of key words, from the plainest construction of a passage to its deepest interpretation, from a recognition of its reference to a testing of its truth. To learn to do all this, that is, to learn to read texts of all sorts is...education in the prime sense."

The Writing Problem is closely allied to The Reading Problem.

The formula: write write write, correct correct correct, grade grade grade — tries to take by storm what can be won only as the result of a slowly ripening response to literary art and linguistic usage, to much and varied reading.

Learning to write is learning precision and economy of style; it is learning the rules and principles that govern written usage in order to speak in one's own unique voice; it is learning the way of being honest about the relation between words and truth; it is learning to state as is, as ought, as if, convincingly; it is learning to overcome jargon, cliché, and other varieties of neat, colorless, and efficient death.

There is also a world to know. The world catches one's eye, as only a world can. A writer reads the world, his text; and his book, if it be good, is a good reading of it. His art is a way of disputing vital points at issue, of trying his strength.

The ghosts that range the self impersonating the life that language takes to live reassure us because they are so familiar, despite the emptiness of their substance.

Words are capable of being used with intelligence, wit and style, even in their most everyday use. But as with any art or craft when used most significantly, they are a labor of love.

Cultivating a love of this language by addressing the poetry that is in every child (and often expressed spontaneously and unexpectedly) is often the shortest line between its power and the child's use of it. As with other kinds of love, the extraordinary human need we have of the right words may be met by the most ordinary of means; e.g., by learning to listen intently to both the spoken and unspoken resonance and meaning of speech; by learning to read and discuss the works of the masters of the language; but, above all, by learning to care about its expression.

It is the caring that counts. As a painter cares about the color and shape and line of his work, so too a good writer cares about his words conveying their fullness of meaning in their most effective of means.

We usually wish to be able to say what we mean. But there is a better and a worse way of saying it. The better way is also a way of helping ourselves know what we mean.

The art of writing, like the arts of humor or love, cannot be studied as one would study the life cycle of a worm. That's the way a worm would study it. It is a reading, it is a prayer, it is a note to a friend. But it is not a Schoolbook study, unless the human spirit is too.

Teach a child to read better and you will be teaching him to write better and to think better.* Teach him to think better and you will be providing him with the possible means of seeing his world more clearly and in truer perspective. Who would not care to see more clearly if it were his eyesight that was impaired?

The power of words can move the heart, enrich the mind, enlarge the soul. Until Everychild learns the difference in personal terms between the language of words well used and that badly used, he will lack the initial interest that it takes to care about this difference.

Talk about twenty six trombones leading the big parade! If you want another kind of good music, try the twenty six letters of the alphabet, skillfully or artistically

---

* A useful book for the teaching of writing on its most elementary level (in the best sense of the term) is: Strunk, William, Jr. and White, E.B, *The Elements of Style* (New York: The Macmillan Company, 1962).

arranged. Now there's something that a "non-reader" might be taught to care about and maybe even want to learn the wonderful ways those letters work and how to make some music of his own.

In writing that is primarily objective — an accurate, economic, grammatical description of a thing or transaction — e.g., a good business letter — the form is direct, logical, impersonal, prescribed by its purpose.

But the writing that is intended to be an expression of the writer's feelings, values, personal experience, has no proper "form" other than his grasp of truth and whatever integrity of language he commands.

The best writing combines both the objective and the personal, both learning and passion, both "real toads" and a deep commitment to the "imaginary garden" in which we find them.

The student has no place to begin but himself and his own limited grasp of the language. Good reading will give him a feeling for the words — What a delight, a teaching, the way that Dickens plays on and with the language! — but the student can learn to write well only through a long apprenticeship in cultivating an intimacy between the language of words and the song of himself.

In poetry — perhaps above all other reading — he will learn the discipline of thought and the exultation of song in one. He will learn — what would be to Monsieur Jourdin's even greater astonishment — that we speak poetry in our more living speech.

If the English language is the flowering, so to speak, of liberal education, English poetry is the lily of the bunch. And if the sickness of the School system is most pronounced and most critical in the teaching and learning of English, there is no mystery as to why poetry was the first part of the English curriculum to fester.

Poetry is a rhythm, precision and conciseness of language, encompassing its richest meaning and associations. ("Poetry," wrote Flaubert, "is as precise as geometry.") Referring to the time when children were taught to commit poetry to memory ("Rote" is the pejorative term that covers a multitude of educational virtues), an editorial in a literary review declares: "Unlike many modern children, they had something elegant, precise and significant to fall back upon: they had their models of wit or feeling, of reflection or passion, of foolishness or wisdom. They had indeed their touchstones of taste."

What are the schools using these days for touchstones of taste? If they were interested, as they should be, in teaching their students something of the power of language that a good poem exhibits, what better way than teaching them how to read good poetry?

By getting to know, from the First Grade, the most powerful sources of linguistic power, the student might acquire the means of following in hot pursuit. Who can doubt that Everychild has the potential power of the primary language in him, and that a real education would help him develop it?

The study of any liberal art is a minor study apart from its works of genius. But the study of history (which is taken here as a prototype of studies in the social order), like the study of imaginative literature, is especially dependent upon the quality of writing in which the study is made, the power of whose language alone can penetrate to even a semblance of historical reality.

History must be learned primarily by the use of books or other reading material because this is the principal means by which knowledge of it is transmitted. The ability to come to terms with words is an historical necessity because an existential one.

Works of history should be selected on the same basis as the rest of the program; namely, that they are the best of their kind.

However, this principle presents a particular difficulty in devising an appropriate history segment for the education of young children.

The limitations of childhood modify the child's understanding at every point, and in social studies that understanding matures especially late. To learn to read, beyond acquisition of the mere rudiments of reading, is to learn to make judgments that are not only intellectual in nature. We read with our hearts as well as with our minds; with the joy and sorrow of our lives, as well as with the discipline of rational faculties that a good education nurtures.

The literature of history has no children's branch, as does imaginative literature. The best preparation for the kind of reading that a school student will or should be doing at the latter stages of a curriculum, in the study of history as well as in the other social studies, is learning to read well in subjects which he can be taught at the preceding stages.

The introductory stage of the study of history would stress the importance of looking up geographical references as they are encountered in reading of any kind; of learning to read a map; of studying the crucial connection between geography and history, which is not only an important junction of scientific and non-scientific (i.e., historical) knowledge, but also illustrates the significant difference between these two kinds of knowledge.

Classroom discussion in which children expound their views upon what the President should do about poverty, crime, or foreign policy are only a parody of serious inquiry. "In the first and second grade," writes Maurie Hillson, editor,

Elementary Education, "economics is being enjoyed and assimilated in a meaningful way by many very young children." The School approach is absolutely fearless about the teaching of any subject at any level, provided only that it is guaranteed not to be taught seriously.

Although education looks to the individual work of liberal art as the right material for its purposes — because it is there that the language is to be found in which the subject finds its most characteristic, most genuine, most powerful expression — it is, however, in the nature of childhood to be excluded from understanding those matters in which there can be no readiness until there is ripeness.

Where are the frames of reference in childhood — the moral experience, the intellectual and emotional maturity, the historical perspective, the political knowledge — that would make serious questions of social policy accessible to children?

The entire range of significant connections in any subject worth studying is more than any teacher is capable of communicating to any significant depth. A choice must be made among the inexhaustible number of topics or connections possible. The problem is not unavailability of materials but School unwillingness to use the illustriously appropriate materials that are on hand.

As Martin Mayer suggests in his study of the teaching of social studies in the schools: "Anyone who has read Parkman or Gibbon or Macaulay will find it hard to believe that students learn more history from, say, a textbook...than they would from such authors."

If School textbooks in the social studies are "uniformly dull and without focus, often inaccurate, almost always misleading," as Mayer also says, what is the point of using them? What good purpose is served by teaching history with latterday Parson Weems versions that resurrect a Schoolbook past that is stranger but less honest than good fiction.

Malarkey is not honest; therefore, it cannot educate.

That the study of history proceeds best in the writings of its best historians is, no doubt, a wretched commonplace. But then so is a great deal else that the schools mysteriously reject or neglect.

The double standard of learning — one for School and the other for Education — denies Everychild the right to have his mind taken seriously. If he is to be treated as a serious student — the best way of helping him become one — he is entitled to serious materials of study and to serious standards of excellence.

School history textbooks turn the mind to pap just by being looked upon. And a terrible death of the mind it is to be suffocated between the pap and the malarkey.

Historical writing at its best exemplifies both craftsmanship and genius; both the historian as "technician" and as "artist." The value that a school student would derive from reading a few good examples of the historian's art, when sufficiently matured to read them, would not be that he would thus immediately gain the wisdom to think about world problems realistically, but that he would be beginning his apprenticeship in learning how to read history.

History is part of the knowledge we require of any subject. The historical is the antithesis of the antiquarian consciousness. As an essential part of liberal education, history seeks to extend horizons, to enrich experience, to free the mind of menial influence. History as a liberal art reminds us of memorable occasions. "I shall begin," said Pericles in his funeral oration, "with our ancestors."

We remember the American past that we too, in our own generation, may be free.

If the study of history cannot help us distinguish our friends from our enemies; tell the difference between aggression and defense, dictatorship and democracy, terrorism and anti-terrorism; recognize the connections between freedom and law, justice and economics, peace and military readiness — what good is it?

The study of history provides paradigms of possibility, vicarious experiences that are cautionary, edifying, exemplary, and applicable to what is or may become our own decision-making responsibilities.

Needless to say, we must allow for both individual and collective variability in what we learn from historical studies. Analogies can and must be made in the decision-making process. However, because each historical event is unique, it is essential that all analogies be made with appropriate qualification — tentatively and with some skepticism.

Furthermore, no matter how similar two events may outwardly seem, we are prevented from fully understanding them not only by differences of time and place, by particular social, economic, political, and cultural influences, but also by the inward purpose, value, meaning, with which we as human beings invest our lives.

We remember the past because ours is an historical nature and therefore to forget or grossly distort the meaning of the history with which we identify ourselves is to be cut off from our own reality.

We remember the past partly because we want to remember it as an essential part of ourselves and partly because we cannot help remembering and being influenced by it.

The writing of history is a form of persuasion, and we are less persuaded by the historical facts than by their interpretation. The facts are essential, but they become significant only when significantly composed.

What, for example, should we learn from so large an historical fact as World War I? That war is horrible? This was no secret before 1914. That war is "meaningless?" The horror of war doesn't persuade us of this. A man who fights to prevent his death or enslavement is in no different moral case than a people or a nation that does the same. We are able to learn as much from a small as from a large historical fact — which suggests that it is not the size of the event but the size and validity of the interpretation that counts for understanding.

In World War II six million Jews and millions of non-Jews were murdered by the Nazis. How is this "simple" fact to be understood? What is the "lesson" to be learned from it?

Obviously, one lesson to be learned from history is the lesson of power. Lacking military power, the European Jews were annihilated; possessing military power, the Israelis save themselves from annihilation. Could any historical lesson be clearer?

But just as obviously, power is not its own justification. Power is an instrument of political policy; it is an indispensable instrument of all the politics of human life. The study of history enables us to trace the causes and effects of power struggles. It may also help us to distinguish between power and authority; that is, the use of force that does not have moral justification and that which does.

The writing of history that is abstracted from a moral context fails to persuade us of its importance because it fails to satisfy the sense with which we experience the quality of historical events in our own lives; namely, that their meaning is bound up with the extent to which, as we understand them, they degrade, sadden, and do injury to human life; or strengthen, gladden, and purify it.

"Sympathy is a form of knowledge," wrote R. H. Tawney. "It cannot be taught. It can only be absorbed by association with those the depth of whose natures has enabled them most profoundly to feel and most adequately to express it."

A study of history that strives merely to be "objective" cannot come to grips with its reality. Historical issues derive their significance from patterns of value at stake. What could we learn from a history of the American Civil War that found good "reasons" for both the justification and the condemnation of slavery, nicely balanced — except a distortion of history?

The merit of a particular work of history depends not only upon its logical rigor; its fairness of judgment; its selection, evaluation, and structuring of relevant facts; but also its point of view, its philosophy, upon which all the foregoing depend — and of course upon the quality of language empowering any work of literary art.

In the education of Everychild, we want the reading of historians who are faithful to and have an eye for the cogent facts; who possess the art of writing well — but who are not moral eunuchs.

The more valid meanings of history are those established not by bloodless analogy or sterile "objectivity" but by passionate identity — the identity of value and conviction and memory.

This is the meaning of history that is most meaningful. It is not known merely as a cognitive object but by commitment upon which the survival and increase of the self and of the community depend.

History never repeats itself, but the reasons for which men live and die invariably do.

What is science?

It is an interpretation of "nature" — the world accessible to the senses but existing in and independently of them; it is also the hypothesis, however arrived at — hunch, chance, dreams, logic — that underlies this interpretation.

It is a tacit agreement among scientists that the result of their investigations shall be verified in accordance with certain conventional procedures; it is also the language with which these results are described.

It is looking at evidence with a coldly rational mind; it is also the seeking of evidence with a passionately self-centered heart.

Science is what a scientist *qua* biologist, physicist, chemist, or any other suitably nomenclatured person, does. Its limits are those circumscribed by man's nature, society, and history, as well as by physical reality itself.

Despite the fact (or perhaps because of it) that we know much more about that "great undiscovered ocean of truth" than Newton did, it appears much more formidable to us than it did to him. To him it was "undiscovered"; to us, in the last analysis, undiscoverable.

What Science Knows is no longer above suspicion. There is a worm in its epistemological bud.

The history of scientific ideas is a history of changing concepts. "Thus, a theory is converted," wrote Professor Joseph Schwab in his Inglis lecture, *The Teaching of Science as Enquiry*, "not into 'fact', but into another theory, another which is more complete, more coherent, more comprehensive. And the process of conversion is not likely to end until science finds one theory which will embrace all data about all subject matters — a termination to be sought but hardly likely to be found." Compared with the longevity of philosophic and religious wisdom, scientific truth is to be classified with the ephemeral of human understanding. Sufficient unto the day are the scientific truths thereof.

The Nobel laureate in physics Polykarp Kusch writes: "A large number of theories of science have enjoyed a considerable success because both the simple statements of the theory and the predictions of the theory were demonstrably consistent with the available body of observational data. As new observations were made or as the consequences of the theory were explored in greater depth, inconsistencies with observation were found. Either the theory had to be discarded, as was Newton's particle theory of light under the pressure of new observations; or the region of applicability of the theory had to be formally delimited, as for classical mechanics with the birth of the special theory of relativity."

The further man extends his scientific knowledge and the more he gains upon that undiscovered ocean of scientific truth, the narrower and more alien seems the margin of the shore. "Our present relation to the world," wrote Buber, "resembles that told in Egyptian myth of the relation to the god whose secret names one has learned, which knowledge one may use like a bundle of powers. The basic mathematical formulae agree, a kind of symbol at once abstract and practical; experiment confirms it; but now for the first time the uncanny strangeness of the world is perceived."

Science begins by taking thought; but, fallen into the clutches of technological application, it ends by lapsing into mindlessness. The Perfect Butler. Send a man to the moon? — Sir, at once. — Take out a city? —Sir, it is done.

Simple science, ignorant of or indifferent to reality other than its own, is a form of sophisticated idiocy, the steadily increasing and uncontrolled power of which could only one day eliminate mankind in a fit of abstraction.

What science is and how it should be understood are questions of the greatest significance to education. That science is one of the humanities must not only be admitted but insisted upon. However, science that claims its truth is the only one that is knowable, or that is worth knowing, begins by being a-humanistic and ends by being anti-human.

A liberal education would emphasize the fact that science is not done in a personal and historical vacuum. It would pay some attention to the influences that political, social, and economic facts have upon scientific discovery.

Science shares with its companion liberal arts the use of language as the instrument of its understanding. Works of scientific genius contribute to scientific knowledge and are exemplars of scientific thinking for exactly the same reason: science takes place at its best in the most powerful expression of its thought. The opinion that in science education the quality of language is not important as long as the facts are conveyed is educational schizophrenia. The language is of the essence. "As the language of a poet rings with a truth that eludes the clumsy explanations of his commentators," writes Sir Arthur Eddington, "so the geometry of relativity in its perfect harmony expresses a truth of form and type in nature, which my bowdlerized version misses."

The gross misunderstanding of science resulting from the belief that the committees who write the School textbooks communicate the same science in their versions as do the classics of scientific literature in theirs is the price that the schools pay for using an inferior language of their own.

Whether or not the "facts" of science are true — true today, they may well be untrue tomorrow. Biological science, it is said, now doubles its significant knowledge every ten to fifteen years. A principal value attributed to textbooks is that they are current. But the teaching of science as a liberal art is one current that School textbooks cannot step into even once.

Science is no exception to the rule that style is blood brother to substance. The language of a work of liberal art is the imprint of its artist. In the work of its great writers and thinkers, the student comes to grips with science at its most scientific.

Has an acknowledged masterpiece of scientific thought anything of importance to communicate once its findings have been superseded? This is the crucial test of science as a liberal art.

"What was a masterpiece in 1939 [Linus Pauling's *The Nature of the Chemical Bond*] declares an article on the scientific textbook, "is just another book on the subject in 1960. So even here the importance of content is over-riding and the history of the literature of science must be considered as a qualitatively different study from the history of literature, in that the value of a scientific work is sharply dependent on time."

But apparently it is not all that different; in fact, hardly different at all. For the writer of this article goes on to describe the quality of writing in Professor Pauling's book as "pedestrian." A pedestrian style is indeed "sharply dependent on time," regardless of its subject; it lives only as long as its ideas and information are new and of practical interest.

Gay Wilson Allen, the biographer of William James, writes: "When he published his massive *Principles of Psychology* in 1892, after twelve years of labor on it, James himself predicted that as a contribution to science the book would soon be out of date. He was right; but the *Principles* is still almost universally considered the fullest and best work on the subject published before the twentieth century and has survived as literature though its science has long since become archaic."

But, furthermore, how could the literature of science be "qualitatively different" from any other kind of literature? The integrity of language is no respecter of subjects. Science is under the same dispensation as any other subject that the language of words expresses; and, therefore, has the same capability of enduring beyond its conclusions as any other.

Science too exists in the integrity of its language, and in that integrity shares a perennial element with all the other various forms of literature.

In the foreword to the Anchor edition of Darwin's *The Voyage of the Beagle*, the annotator of the work, Leonard Engel, writes: "It is not only one of the great classics of natural history and a key work in the evolution of modern thought; it is also first-rate as literature" — three good criteria for the selection of writings in scientific literature at any level of education.

The School textbook approach abstracts science from a humanistic context;

lacking art, it lacks — in its best sense — science also. It interposes its interpretations between the student and the scientists; makes scientific thought seem cut-and-dried (divided into segregated, sterile units); obscures the perplexity of the problem and nullifies the excitement of the search; and performs an educational lobotomy on the subject, so that its characteristic life is destroyed.

The individual work is the form of the subject that matters most, in science or in any other liberal art. In its essence the "subject" is the precise way in which its best thought is expressed. This form is the style of its power. Change it and you make its study something else.

The President's Commission on Foreign Languages and International Studies reported that foreign language study in elementary school has "virtually disappeared" and that only 15 percent of U. S. high school students study a foreign language today.

The study of a foreign language ought to be based not upon fugitive, private, or incidental consideration, but upon direct relation to the aims of the entire liberal arts program.

As there are particular works of literary, mathematical, musical, and visual art conspicuous for their appropriateness as materials of study in liberal education; so, too, there are foreign languages.

The study of a classical language (Latin or Greek) brings to the present the reality of the past and thus helps the student understand better the roots of his own culture. It enables him to examine objectively and from a certain distance, as it were, the structure of his own language. "The exercise, day after day," wrote W. H. Auden, "of translating into and out of classical languages...taught me to understand the nature of my native tongue as no other method, I believe, could have done."

The study of a modern foreign language gives the student a deeper understanding of the thought and feeling of another contemporary people. Both classical and modern foreign languages can and should be gateways to their literature.

These frequently-cited reasons for foreign language study also suggest criteria for deciding the particular foreign languages to be included as part of an elementary liberal education.

"The elements of Latin," wrote Whitehead, "exhibit a peculiarly plain concrete case of language as a structure...In English, French, and Latin we possess a triangle....This is the essential triangle of literary culture, containing within itself freshness of contrast, embracing both the present and past....Exactness, definiteness, and independent power of analysis are among the main prizes of the whole study."

That these prizes are conspicuously lacking in the School's teaching of English undoubtedly accounts for a great deal of the widespread dismay over the inability of American students to use even their native language well.

Listening, speaking, reading, writing, is the order in which a child learns English. He speaks spontaneously with the patterns he has acquired by imitation and by the exercise of his own language-making faculty. A child learning French or any other modern foreign language who follows the same order would achieve similar results. A student who begins French in the first grade and continues it throughout the entire course of this program will have a good conversational and reading command of it by the time he graduates at age sixteen. As conversational and reading ability develop, the student will in time be reading books in French on or near the level of his reading in English.

The study of French grammar should be held to a minimum and included only as incidentally necessary to strengthen and purify conversation and reading, developing naturally and inductively from these activities and toward the written use of the language.

In the present climate of educational opinion and practice, French for Everychild may seem eccentric but within tolerable limits of eccentricity. But to advocate the teaching of Latin for all school students must seem, if not incomprehensible, at least absurd.

However, the question is, How to be serious about the teaching of language? If suggesting the study of Latin for Everychild appears an extravagant notion, is this because there are indeed better ways to study and acquire the discipline of good language usage? Present educational results — or lack of them — suggest that whatever these ways are, the schools have not found them.

Does the benefit of studying Latin justify the time and effort? This depends of course on the objectives of the program and on what other ways these might be achieved more efficiently.

Latin is the "pattern literary language." (Saintsbury) If studying the structure of another language enables us to understand our own better, it seems appropriate that this language should be one that, like Latin, is compatible in so many ways with the rest of a liberal arts curriculum.

> "The English vocabulary," wrote Wilson Follett in *Modern American Usage*, "besides having hundreds of Latin words taken over *literatim*, consists so preponderantly of Romance elements that the reader equipped with some Latin will understand at sight a great many words of which another cannot make head or tail without a dictionary; and of course even a nodding acquaintance with this dead language opens the way to picking up a reading knowledge of French or Italian. Among the classics of English literature a large number are the work of authors who read (and sometimes wrote) Latin

like their native tongue. Whom more characteristically English than Milton, Dryden, Swift, Dr. Johnson— and yet how full their minds and works of Latin speech and form of thought. It would be rash to maintain that the connection between their powers and their knowledge was accidental. Certainly one still hears of students to whom the hang of their native English suddenly became clear when they began to learn Latin grammar. For the analytic method of grammar appears all the more clearly in a language where inflections show the function of the word in the sentence, and where meaning is not so immediate as to make the form negligible. *If there exists a better pedagogic device than Latin for showing how the Western Languages work, it has not yet been found."* (Emphasis added)

Latin offers a peculiarly apt example of a subject that would seem out of place in almost any other than a liberal arts curriculum, but right in its element within it.

Latin would help strengthen the study of language in the schools exactly where it is now most weak and vulnerable: in its use and understanding of written language.

For nearly two thousand years Latin was the principal written language of the West. As the second foreign language in the curriculum, it would not only have much value for linguistic reasons, but also for the development of historical awareness.

In the study of language there is no issue between essential trivia and significant ideas, as there is none between the technique and the substance of its art. But there is an issue between the better and the worse ways that technique and trivia on the one hand, and substance and meaning on the other, can be studied in relation to each other. The conjugation and declension of Latin words in isolation from linguistic principles, literary examples, and the human values bound up with the integrity of human speech, are not a study in liberal art but an exercise in illiberal sterility. Liberal education studies the forms of language, but language understood as a history, an excellence, and a unique characteristic of the human spirit.

If teaching Latin to underprivileged or culturally disadvantaged children should appear as being the farthest remove from their "real" needs, this could be said just as well of any foreign language; indeed, of mathematics, of poetry, of music, and of most arts that comprise a liberal education.

But the mind is not cultivated any differently on one side of the railroad tracks than on the other; or among the dark-skinned than among the pink and grey; or, for that matter, among the "bright" than among those apparently endowed with only ordinary talent or aptitude for learning. The proper care and feeding of the mind doesn't admit the rule that the better the mind the greater its need for a good diet.

An article in U. S. News and World Report, surveying the ignorance of foreign languages in this country, declares: "Hundreds of elementary schools have introduced Latin to inner-city pupils who read English below grade level. Philadelphia offers Latin to 16,000 students in grades four to six. Los Angeles started similar classes four years ago...."

The curriculum specialist for classic languages in the Philadelphia schools, declared that: "Pupils at the fifth grade level advanced one full year in standardized vocabulary test scores, compared with pupils with similar backgrounds who got no Latin."

The idea that a learning skill can be transferred from one subject to another has long been in the academic doghouse. But the validity or non-validity of this idea would appear to depend a great deal upon what is being transferred to what. A growing body of test data clearly shows the beneficial effects of Latin study upon English language skills.*

In the program being described in this book, Everychild would begin his Latin studies in the eighth grade when his analytical powers have reached an appropriate stage of development and would continue them for two or three years.

As the rudiments of syntax are the key to how Latin as a written language works; so, too, the study of its literature (particularly its poetry) is the key to the genius of the language, which the student would study for its own sake as well of course as the key to classical culture and its influence.

"Any language," wrote Edmund Wilson, "that has once borne the impress of the masters of thought and art is impregnated forever after with the genius and authority of these masters."

Language is shaped in the response of spirit to the possibilities and necessities of existence. It is possible to study a language only linguistically; but given half a chance its literature will out, and in its literature its genius and its humanity.

By learning to use foreign languages, Everychild will learn to use his own language with greater precision. He may even, through the power of literature, gain a better understanding of himself and of the world in which he lives.

*For further information about the teaching of Latin in the schools write: National Commitee for Latin and Greek c\o Robert La Bouve, 5804 Back Court Dr., Austin, TX 78731

Chapter VII
THE STUDY OF MATHEMATICS AS A LIBERAL ART

> And one of the main reasons which keep those who are
> beginning these studies [of geometry] out of the
> true road they ought to follow is the notion
> they get at the start that the good things
> are inaccessible because they bear
> the names: great, high, exalted,
> sublime, That spoils
> everything.
>
> Blaise Pascal

Pure mathematics and applied mathematics were the Siamese twins that non-Euclidean geometry cut asunder, thus liberating the power of each to go its own distinctive way, still related but no longer bound.

The statements of mathematics and of its applications refer to two distinct realms of meaning: the former, logical or hypothetical; the latter, physical or empirical. No single term expresses both realms in one univocal meaning.

Pure mathematics occurs in Ruritania; it devises proofs of a world of its own; it is the very model of apodictic generality. But the statements of applied mathematics — which function to "measure every wand'ring planet's course," or whatever else is quantitatively ascertainable — are subject to all the imperfections, imprecisions, and uncertainties inherent in measurement and observation.

"What has to be grasped by all who are interested in education," writes the noted mathematician Marshall H. Stone, "is that our conception of the nature of mathematics has been revolutionized....Mathematics is now seen to have no necessary connections with the physical world beyond the vague and mystifying one implicit in the statement that thinking takes place in the brain. The discovery that this is so may be said without exaggeration to mark one of the most significant intellectual advances in the history of mankind, comparable so far as mathematics is concerned with only one other great discovery — the recognition by the Greeks that the empirical facts of geometry fall into logical patterns which can be so amalgamated that the whole subject appears as a coherent logical structure based on a limited number of axioms."

If the patterns of pure mathematics are purely logical and have "no necessary connections" with physical reality, how then does the external world of physical reality appear to obey them? Natural phenomena do not of course "obey" these patterns, but some mathematical models coincide with and apply cogently to part of the physical structure of reality as we are able to observe and measure them.

Every scientific "law" can be interpreted in mathematical terms; but, needless to say, not every set of mathematical equations can be demonstrated to predict or coincide with a scientific law. "If mathematical models were judged in terms of the dichotomy, right or wrong, they all would be wrong; the real world is far too complex to be represented accurately by anything but the analogue computer COSMOS. Models must be evaluated along a spectrum from good to bad according to the validity and usefulness of the predications based on them..." (Cambridge Conference on School Mathematics)

Mathematical signs do not express the signs of nature in a one-to-one correspondence. Physical reality — or, for that matter, any realm of order; social phenomena, visual art, music — can be read "mathematically," but mathematical signs coincide exactly only with their own non-empirical reality.

Pure mathematics achieves its validity apart from either the knowledge of natural phenomena or the aims of social utility. Technology achieves its validity only by means of this knowledge and because of these aims. Science stands midway between mathematics and technology. Like mathematics, science *qua* science is indifferent to utilitarian (i.e. social) aims, and, like technology, is empiric in nature.

Both science and technology are dependent upon mathematics, but in different ways. Mathematics serves science by generating models of order that may suggest empirical patterns; it serves technology by the measurements that mathematical models make possible.

The logical certainty that can be known only in its hypothetical state is the poetry that is lost in translating mathematics into its applications. Functioning only in the world of the logically consistent, mathematics is a reservoir of meaning for the world of the contingent, concrete, controversial, and cluttered.

When the American mathematician C. J. Keyser declared in a lecture, "I have not spoken of 'Applied Mathematics', and that for the best of reasons: there is, strictly speaking, no such thing," he was emphasizing the necessity to keep a decent epistomological distance between mathematical and empirical reality. The relationship between them is clearly a delicate one; and if mathematics, like Ophelia, "is a little mad," as Whitehead wrote (a "refuge from the goading urgency of contingent happenings"), the mathematician or physicist, like Ophelia, has occasion to think himself sorely tried in making connection between two principles of order so insistently distinctive and so unpredictably consistent.

There be four things wonderful to behold; yea, five of which account must be taken: the external reality, the mathematical model, the scientific concept, the measuring instrument, and the fallibility of man.

Whichever came first, pure or applied mathematics — which is cause and which effect, which origin and which development — each is inconceivable without the other, though they function in different realms of meaning. In order to count, there is needed a mathematical system for counting. But how could this develop except out of the practice of counting?

Carl C. Hempel writes that, "no empirical 'basis' or evidence whatever is needed to establish the truth of the propositions of arithmetic." But, declares John Von Neumann, "Mathematical ideas originate in empirics, although the genealogy is sometimes long and obscure. But once they are so conceived, the subject begins to live a peculiar life of its own and is better compared to a creative one, governed by almost entirely aesthetical motivations, than to anything else and, in particular, to an empirical science."

To discern analogies that belong to pure mathematics signifies the power of framing general concepts, which is part of what we mean by human intelligence. Such analogies are in the nature of what it means to count. Whitehead observes that "The first man who noticed the analogy between a group of seven fishes and a group of seven days made a notable advance in the history of thought. He was the first man who entertained a concept belonging to the science of pure mathematics."

If the same term, "seven," be used to express the property of number in more than one set of seven objects, then there is evidenced the peculiar power of thought associated with pure mathematics.

But in one sense at least, things can be "counted" without what is usually meant by a system of counting. Koehler's experiments with birds demonstrated that they are capable of distinguishing quantitative differences between separate groups — "thinking in un-named numbers."

Although it is possible to "count" (depending upon what is meant by the term) without a counting system, counting as men count, not as birds — or performing any other operation of applied mathematics — requires a mathematical model; that is, a logical order of thought analogous to observations in the empirical order.

If the "locus" of applied mathematics is the external world, where is the mathematical reality that is the locus of pure mathematics?

The cultural anthropologist Leslie A. White takes issue with the assertion of the English mathematician and philosopher G. H. Hardy, that "mathematical reality lies outside us." Professor White contends that mathematical reality is wholly cultural: "The sort of reality possessed by a code of etiquette, traffic regulations, the rules of baseball, the English language or rules of grammar."

If the terms of the statement "two plus two equal four" are logically irrefutable and even tautological, then this statement leaves no room for a difference of opinion, as there surely must be in interpreting the other instances of cultural phenomena cited by Professor White.

In response to the question as to how the concepts of mathematics originated before there was a cultural tradition, White declares: "To be sure, the first mathematical ideas to exist were brought into being by the nervous system of individual human beings. They were, however, exceedingly simple and rudimentary. Had it not been for the human ability to give these ideas overt expression in symbolic form and to communicate them to one another so that new combinations would be formed...the human species would have made no mathematical progress beyond its initial stage."

This may well be. "Had it not been...." That is to say, human culture is dependent upon the facts of human nature; and these facts being as they are, men are enabled to construct languages, the language of mathematics among them.

Professor White argues "that all of mathematics is nothing more than a particular kind of primate behavior." However, if the first man to express himself on the statement that "two plus two equal four" had come to another conclusion than the one usually given, one would suppose that his fellow primates might have thought him eccentric; or, perhaps, idiotic — that is, using a private language of his own.

Professor White refers the reader to the example of anthropoid apes to demonstrate how mathematical ideas originate outside a cultural tradition. "They are exceedingly intelligent and versatile. They have a fine appreciation of geometric forms, solve problems by imagination and insight, and possess not a little originality."

No one would be so crude as to want to demean an ape's appreciation of geometric forms. But this argument obscures the fact that it is precisely because of man's language faculty and its power of symbolic abstraction that he is not only able to transmit and develop mathematical ideas but also to conceive them in the first place.

The inability of the ape to transmit mathematical culture is based on the simple fact that it has none. If mathematics is neither for birds nor for apes, but is found only in human culture (although its "reality" is not necessarily confined therein), then it is clearly to the nature of man and his culture that we must look for a possible answer to Professor White's question (which goes back twenty-five hundred years to Phythagoras): "Do mathematical truths reside in the external world, there to be discovered by man, or are they man-made inventions?" — an answer that finds the locus of mathematical reality neither simply to "lie outside us" (pi in the sky), nor, as White puts it, to be "a part of human *culture*, nothing more." [Italics his]

If mathematical reality is really "nothing more" than human culture, from where does the ape get the "appreciation of geometric forms" attributed to it? Surely not from man?

In the last analysis, we cannot know the extent to which "mathematical truths reside in the external world" because — there can be no "last" analysis. We cannot know the extent to which the patterns of mathematics coincide with the ultimate physical structure of the universe until we have discovered this structure, until we know all of physical reality that there is to know, until there are no longer new observations of the world that man can make.

In the ancient world Arithmetica and Logistca were the terms that roughly distinguished pure from applied mathematics. The New Math was interpreted as a kind of Back to Arithmetica movement. In fact, however, School appears never to have made up its mind as to the primary purpose of this "new" mathematics. It emphasized structure and concepts at the same time that it selected as bearers of these the topics that were considered of greatest utility in a scientific and technological society.

New Math became a halfway station — leaving the student outside the substantially practical and not yet arrived at the significantly liberal.

The School mathematics curriculum appears to be little shaped by a commanding principle. If the New Math failed to achieve its purpose, it is not because of lack of co-operation given it by the schools or because parents opposed it or because teachers could not be trained to teach it; but because the understanding of its purpose had been inappropriate, uncertain, or ambivalent.

In School environs the "practical" brand almost invariably wins. The increasing interest in computers is typical. But according to which principles of practicality are mathematical topics to be selected? Practical in relation to what? How practical can the study be when it is separated from its possible practice — and even this possibility applicable to only a small fraction of the total student population — by light years of childhood?

If the practical value of mathematics is taken, like the "truth" of the axioms, as self-evident; or if it is seen primarily as an anticipation of future vocational needs, it will only seem a senseless imposition to most students.

Moreover, the genuinely practical purpose is only really well-served where there first has been laid a strong conceptual foundation. The dilemma is, however, that because of the extremely abstract nature of mathematics, no such foundation can be laid for it in early childhood education. Children are not strong conceptual thinkers. If a liberal arts education means the encounter with what is characteristic of the best that language has to offer, then mathematics cannot be studied as a liberal art by most children until about the seventh or eighth grade.

However, there are no compelling reasons, practical or theoretical, for children prior to this age making extensive investigations into the structure or foundations of mathematics. And since in any case, they cannot study these prior to this time in first-rate works, what is the value or necessity of studying them in juvenile versions?

In its emphasis on structure, concepts, and foundations, the New Math exemplifies Professor Jerome S. Bruner's well-known aphorism that: "Any subject can be taught effectively in some intellectually honest form to any child at any stage of development."

Anything, so this viewpoint goes, can be digested to make some kind of sense in one form or other to somebody.

"The task of teaching a subject to a child at any particular age.," says Professor Bruner, "is one of representing the structure of that subject in terms of the child's way of viewing things."

One might gather from this that it would not be possible to teach a child the meaning of the idea of tragedy in an "intellectually honest form" until he is old enough to feel the pity and terror represented in the great tragedies of dramatic literature. Pathos and sorrow certainly exist in children's literature, but the idea of a "tragic fall," in its full moral and spiritual significance, demands a comprehension of the height and depth of human existence that is completely outside a child's experience.

Not so, according to Bruner. "If it is granted, for example," he says, "that it is desirable to give children an awareness of human tragedy and a sense of compassion for it, is it not possible at the earliest appropriate age to teach the literature of tragedy in a manner that illuminates but does not threaten?"

But if one does not feel threatened by the pity and terror, where is the sense of tragedy?

"Any of the great literary forms can be handled in the same way....So too in science," writes Bruner. And so too in every subject, the student is handed up from grade to grade — missing the point of his education at every level. (Does any child ever believe that School and he are at the same place at the same time?)

Young children can't understand the substance of tragedy; therefore, no necessity exists for them to grasp its "structure" in some diluted form or content. The educational necessity, embodied in the curriculum, to understand a structure comes into being only at the point where it can be understood in a context of language that does justice to its meaning.

There is a "spiral" effect that occurs when the student is introduced to a continuing development of the same concept as he advances in its study. The student will thus be engaged from the first grade in reading and discussing some of the same themes throughout the entire course of his liberal education — indeed, throughout the entire course of his life.

However, this kind of approach deepens the student's understanding of these concepts by means of works that are of greater intellectual and imaginative power than merely to provide an occasion for the comprehension of "structure" or only to serve as a preparation for more sophisticated learning.

When the Cambridge Conference on School Mathematics declared that: "Concepts like set, function, transformation group, and isomorphism can be introduced in rudimentary form to very young children, repeatedly applied until a sophisticated comprehension is built up," a spiral method of this kind invariably suggests to the student that his learning at any one stage is merely to prepare him for a stage higher up. He is taught "informal" geometry in the early grades, and then taught it again and again later on. The student acquires an exaggerated case of *deja vu* before he encounters his education — if he ever does — in its truest presence. He receives nothing in its original state; it is all second-hand and often shoddy at that — a Goodwill Industries education — which hardly seems the way to build up "sophisticated comprehension".

Re-reading a first-rate work makes educational sense. But textbook learning "repeatedly applied" only makes school seem to the average student like nothing so much as a treadmill.

As fundamental as the distinction between pure and applied mathematics — and following directly from it — is the distinction that must be made between the study of mathematics as a liberal art and the study of its practical use in science and technology. Since applied mathematics has to do with the empirical world, it is more meaningfully studied in relation to and as an extension of this world than in textbook units divorced from both its practical context and its historical development.

The topics of School mathematics stand in precarious isolation — but tenuously related to each other, but faintly recognizable as part of a great intellectual tradition, and culminating in some usefulness but by happenstance.

By what principle shall it be determined which of these topics are of most worth? Clearly, the topics that are of importance for one kind of utility will not be of equal importance according to other kinds. Where it is not mathematics *per se*, but its applications, that are the focus of interest, these should be studied in the context of their use.

Mathematics relates to science or technology at the point where it can be demonstrated that a theorem applies to a particular segment of physical reality and it is of practical use or necessity to know the extent to which it applies. The mathematics that must be known at this point is determined by non-mathematical considerations. It is in relation to these, as the need develops in the later course of the student's more specialized technological training, that the requisite mathematical topics should be pursued.

Mathematics is both a utilitarian and a liberal art. The study of mathematics as a liberal art in the latter part of elementary education doesn't concern itself directly with the utility of mathematics. But it is hardly possible for those who favor its liberal study to be unaware of or indifferent to the use of mathematics in science, industry, and technology, any more than those who see the study of mathematics primarily in terms of its applied use are likely to be ignorant or unappreciative of its purely theoretical or artistic value also.

"Since, then, mathematics is an entirely free activity, unconditioned by the external world, it is more just to call it an art than a science. It is as independent as music of the external world; and although, unlike music, it can be used to illuminate natural phenomena, it is just as 'subjective', just as much of a product of the free creative imagination....The literature of mathematics is full of aesthetic terms and the mathematician who said that he was less interested in results than in beauty of the methods by which he found the results was not expressing an unusual sentiment." (J. W. N. Sullivan)

Like much else in education, the problem of choosing between the utilitarian and the liberal values of mathematics is primarily one of timing and emphasis. The liberal approach to the study of mathematics ought to take precedence, at least chronologically, if for no other reason than that the liberal use enhances the practical.

But, furthermore, when the practical value of mathematics is emphasized from the beginning as the principal, if not exclusive, reason for learning it, its study as a liberal art cannot help but seem an intrusion; irrelevant, mystifying, burdensome — lacking in substance and reality, like a ghost. No wonder so many students find it hard to believe that its study matters.

The purpose of mathematical study in schools is not the training of boy engineers or girl scientists. Nothing is more antiquated than yesterday's progressivism. It was not so long ago that retail transactions and other such homely life adventures seemed to the school authorities to be New. But as a motivational force the indisputably Promethean powers of mathematical application leave most school students cold. "The student is bribed," wrote John G. Kemeny, former Chairman, U. S. Commission of Mathematics Instruction (and former president of Dartmouth), "into taking an interest by promises that Mathematics will turn out to be useful in getting correct change or building pyramids or making atomic bombs." If the student has to be converted to mathematics by its utility, he is sure to be a non-believer.

What interests a student in mathematics is determined by the same principle that applies to all his studies. The mind is most interested in — and the self most deeply engaged by — what uses it best.

The validity of this principle of learning is not necessarily negated by the wealth of exceptions that might appear to apply to it. Perhaps the most obvious exception is that the mind evidences an enormous range of individual differences — differences that are effects of character, temperament, culture, physical condition, opportunity, genes, and chance. A student may clearly be reluctant to learn what is just as clearly good for him.

But quite aside from the exceptions to this general principle is the pervasive fact that the same mind is capable of being used well or poorly, at a lesser or greater degree of capability; and that, in general, the meaning and integrity inherent in the disciplines of liberal art are not only of particular, intrinsic, interest to the mind, but also "naturally" interest it, analogous to the way in which strength and health naturally interest the body.

To be serious in education is neither to force-feed nor to water down (the New Math managed to accomplish both these dubious feats at once), but to bring together the maturity of the student with a comparable maturity of the art.

The New Math textbook may have been better than those that immediately preceded it, but they were still a long way from teaching mathematics as a liberal art, which is the most important reason for studying it. Education should be one place where, whatever else life subsequently holds for the child, he shall have had, at least here, a direct knowledge of the best of its kind.

The mathematics curriculum must, like the other parts of elementary education, be fashioned by considerations suggested by the integrity of the language and by the capability of the student. The primary grades are not the time to begin study of structure and foundations of mathematics, and diluted Schoolbook versions are not the appropriate style of their beginning.

In the New Math the schools, despite their devotion to "readiness," taught or tried to teach, basic concepts of mathematics with what can only be described as indecent haste. The schools use seven-league boots where they might better stroll, and they stroll where there is the possibility of taking great strides.

The student who is allowed to wait until he can study geometry in Euclid has a master for his teacher. What or whom does he have when he studies *Geometry for Second Graders*?

It is the nature of mathematical thought, said Whitehead, that "connections between things are exhibited which, apart from the agency of human reason, are extremely unobvious."

What is the necessity or desirability of presenting to the child "adapted" versions of these connections rather than waiting until he has developed the intellectual maturity to learn some mathematics from its masters — the kind of mathematics that mathematicians mean when they speak of their discipline as a liberal art?

If the purpose of studying mathematics seems obscure sometimes, this may be because its nature is obscure, even to mathematicians. "It is hard to know what you are talking about in mathematics," said James R. Newman, editor of *The World of Mathematics*, "yet no one questions the validity of what you say. There is no other realm of discourse half so queer." Mathematics is of course a realm of discourse and not a distinct language, like music and visual art. It is, however, commonly referred to as a language of its own, and it is sufficiently distinct in the history of ideas and as an academic discipline to warrant separate consideration from the rest of this language.

The study of mathematics appears connected, somehow, both to the nature of the universe and to the student's eventual employment. Having such shining connections, it must be important. However, since the intellectual validity of pure mathematics is secured by neither of these, we must look to other considerations to justify its place in the liberal arts curriculum.

It is not plausible to suppose that mankind is divided by a line on one side of which are those, a select few, who are capable of learning the language of mathematics, and on the other side those — the overwhelming majority — who are not. Contrary to popular superstition, good mathematicians are not more liberally endowed with intelligence and imagination than good poets, good painters, or good musician.

The simple and undeniable fact that there are some students who have an aptitude for mathematics, and some who have not, masks the just as simple and even more significant fact that intelligence functions, in mathematics as elsewhere, to comprehend the intelligible. It is not unreasonable to suppose that if properly taught the student of ordinary intelligence can learn mathematics in accordance with his rational ability, willingness, and opportunity.

But how many are properly taught? Indeed, what is a good mathematical education? If most students dislike and do poorly in mathematics, there is reason to think that the fault may not be theirs. "Mathematics suffers much," wrote the philosopher Scott Buchanan, "but most of all from its teachers. A great many sometime students of mathematics try to persuade themselves that they haven't mathematical minds, when as a matter of fact they have only had non-mathematical teachers."

Under School conditions, it is not difficult to see why only a student with an extraordinary, if enigmatic, aptitude for mathematics should be thought typical of those who achieve any real understanding of the subject and who freely choose to pursue its study beyond the strict call of necessity.

The study and teaching of mathematics are justified by no better reason than that of any other liberal art — the effect of the power, integrity, and beauty of its language on the mind of the student. "We have all met or heard of people of little formal schooling," says Northrop Frye, "who know the Bible and a few English classics and give the impression of essentially educated people. I suggest that the impression is based, not on sentimental illusion, but on the facts of literary education."

Is mathematics education really so different from this? Would not learning to read only a few works of genius in mathematics put the student much more in the way of becoming acquainted with the real article than does a rigmarole of School textbook topics? If these masterworks could not be read with complete comprehension, in their entirety, they could at least be read in part and well enough to make the reading worthwhile.

Mathematics can be taught as a liberal art only with works of liberal art. If the student comes to the most genuine understanding of the other languages of learning in the work of their masters, it is not likely that he will come to a comparable understanding of mathematics in the School textbook presentation of mathematical thought that he now gets.

The computer is School's latest illusion of deliverance from its educational woes.

The development of the computer signaled the start of the technological revolution in the schools. This sign of the times points a way for education to go to the intellectual poorhouse in a style more in keeping with the electronic age. Junk reproduced electronically.

That "computer-controlled instructional systems will revolutionize the teaching-learning process in the years ahead" is undoubtedly good for General Learning Corp. or International Data Inc., but not necessarily good for the education of Everychild.

The school administrator who is confronted by the claim that computer systems will soon be teaching all school subjects is a sitting duck for the sales engineers, management technicians, and computer purveyors, unless he knows exactly what kinds of learning for children he is trying to achieve and what kinds he is not.

"It [computer science] is the fourth basic skill," declared a School Superintendent in Minnesota. The newspaper article in which this statement appears goes on to say that "the pupils in School District 196 are in the vanguard of an educational revolution that is re-defining classroom fundamentals. It is a revolution that could eventually affect the way all children are taught, radically alter the role of the classroom teacher, and in some instances render the teacher unnecessary."

In the present state of educational confusion, it is to be expected that the schools, in coming to rely upon computers to teach their children, will suppose that they do something to improve the student's mind whenever they do something to improve the machine. "Equipped with the newest facilities of engineering," wrote Edgar Wind, "architectural design required of its craftsmen exceptional powers of resistance not to let any of the machinery usurp a function that belongs to the architect himself. The temptation to let the machine have its way increases with the perfection of machinery...." The architect of a design for the education of children should be no less wary of technological gimmicks than the architect of building construction.

The curse of the technician is on the land. How tempting to let Golem do it!

The human spirit is neither a receptacle to be filled nor a clay to be molded. The self may be invited to education, but not coerced; persuaded to it, but not intimidated; led to it, but not manipulated; even seduced by it, but not raped.

A child of six, it is said, is now "exposed" to more facts than a high school graduate of a few decades ago. Computers have their own Parkinson's Law. Facts proliferate in proportion to the power of the machine to produce them. But mere facts have the highest known potentiality for wearying the soul.

In a universe in which the number of facts is innumerable and constantly changing, the quantitative measurement of their acquisition as an index of intellectual progress is, for all practical purposes — meaningless. The problem is to know the facts that are central to the most significant kinds of understanding.

Education "redeems" facts by presenting for consideration the best opinions and ideas, images and premises, about them. How beautiful a mere fact is capable of being! — and how necessary it may be on occasion to establish its validity. But facts must be related to each other in a meaningful pattern. The same "fact" taken from a different perspective may yield a different understanding.

The context in which facts are presented is of crucial importance. Information, knowledge, and understanding are weighted differently in value. Facts divorced from patterns of knowledge are trivial, as knowledge divorced from understanding has no secure foundation.

Facts provide an essential element of learning, but they must be placed within an effective order. Knowledge provides an ordering of facts, but in no vital and compelling relation to human existence. Education needs understanding and wisdom to center it. It needs the marinade of time. Without these how should we sustain ourselves in the universe? How should we tell a curse from a blessing, a time to laugh from a time to weep?

The machine's ability to produce facts is incomparably greater than Everychild's necessity for learning them. The information explosion results, for the most part, in debris. Real education has the effect of making the mind more alive, not burying it. The learning experiences too good to miss are the ones to shape the program.

In elementary education the computer is a fraudulent substitute for a good book and a good teacher — Doctor Faustus with electronic attachments. "Do! Kill thy physician," says Kent to Lear, "and the fee bestow upon the foul disease." At the same time that the technician-salesman is assuring the teaching fraternity at their annual conference that the computer is no substitute for the teacher (why, the teacher is indispensable!) and the teachers are nodding and listening enthralled — he is chopping off their heads.

Although originally the computer manufacturers, salesmem, and technicians assured the School fraternity that it had nothing to fear from the computer in respect to the loss of their jobs, the prospect not only of every classroom but of every home in possession of one of these little devils caused a shift in the sales approach. Now the emphasis is being put upon how much Johnny (and Mary) can learn at home from this technology.

An article on the future of this development looks ahead to the year 2000 when "education in the home is predicted to take over from the primary school teacher." There are many more homes than there are primary schools, a fact which did not require a computer to teach its manufacturers and sales managers.

The computer is a very useful machine for acquiring certain kinds of information; it is invaluable in business and industry, government and the military. But its value in those fields is not the primary objective in the elementary education of children; nor is it noted for its power to develop imagination and intelligence which are the primary objectives of elementary education.

The very power of the computer to solve certain kinds of problems makes it very attractive when getting the "right" answers is the name of the game (and invariably accompanying this approach are the tests and grades considered by the School mentality as the *sine qua non* of education.). But in mathematics education it is less important to teach Everychild how to think like a machine than how to think like a mathematician. "The technological tail must not be allowed to wag the teaching dog."

It is hard to conceive how School could be a more confusing place than it now is — that is, a more certain place for Education to get lost. But if it is possible to conceive this, the computer leads the way to show how it might be done.

"The good teacher," writes Martin Buber, "educates by his speech and by his silence, in the hours of teaching and in the recesses, in casual conversation through his mere existence, only he must be a really existing man and he must be really present to his pupils...."

In genuine education *how* one acquires a fact is at least as important as the fact of acquiring it. The same piece of information received, on the one hand, from a living teacher and, on the other, from a machine — is not the same. Its educational result will be as different as are the living intelligence of a student and the electronic circuit of a stimulus-response robot.

Teaching as liberal art exhibits the worth and the inherent interest of the learning enterprise as no machine (after the initial excitement of pushing buttons wears off) could possibly do. What the teacher teaches, in the context of how he teaches, the kind of person he is, the wit and wisdom with which he illuminates his subject, will be as different in kind from what the student can learn from a computer as School is from Education. It will not necessarily be better in terms of test results; but if test results are the only or the major criterion employed to judge the value of learning, it is School you've got, but not Education.

The more that education — particularly elementary education — becomes cluttered with electronic doo-dads, the less that the little grey cells of the student will be activated. The computer and its attached delusions are only the latest School insult to the minds of our children; educational decadence in its more sophisticated variety.

According to the neo-behaviorist vision of education, life itself is a machine and all that is therein are facts of one kind or another. Once we get it all into the machine (and maybe this little gadget attached to our skulls?), we shall then be able to "think" like a machine. Students in CAI (computer-assisted instruction) are referred to as being "processed." (A computer the machine and Everychild the pigeon.)

Machine-like qualities are the perfect model for a state of School. But where originality and independence, freedom and wisdom, are the qualities a society admires, the way of the *paedagogus ex machina* will be hard.

There are no substitutes, electronic or otherwise, for teachers who are demonstrably competent to teach. A teacher can serve as an example of the way that intelligence functions intelligently and imagination imaginatively; or he can, with his students, read and discuss works of artistic merit in which these qualities are superlatively evidenced. He is, in fact, obliged to do both in relation to each other if he would do either well.

We might be justified in feeling more hopeful about the future of education if we could know that it held a little more seriousness than a portrait of the teacher as a computer-assisted robot; if it held, for example, the seriousness of Everychild learning to read and discuss a good book well.

Insofar as we conceive of education in terms of mental drudgery — donkeywork — we will readily welcome any kind of machine that promises to perform it more efficiently. But a different conception of education would yield a different notion of the kind of teaching that is needed.

The more the art of education is interpreted in neo-behaviorist and "scientific" terms, the more irresistible become the educational claims made on behalf of the computer. As the machine becomes increasingly active in education, the mind of the student becomes increasingly inert; the machine's sophistication becomes the measure of educational progress.

The final triumph of the computer-based approach to education will be to "prove" that there is no essential difference between the "mind" of the machine and the mind of the student. If human intelligence is really no more than a complicated pattern of electronic circuits, maybe some day mankind will discover itself superfluous. It would seem an anti-climax, somehow.

Because School isn't clear about the kind of educational results that are desirable, or how to get those results that clearly are, it is peculiarly vulnerable to the various educational nostrums that are dreamt up from time to time. Where are the educational furbelows of yesteryear? The more that School appears to change, the more it proves not to be Education.

The problem for the school student is not how to master mathematics (Gauss is said to have been the last mathematician to whom this feat could be ascribed), but how to learn to think mathematically about mathematical ideas.

Since what is thought to be "current" in mathematics changes continuously, textbooks must be continuously revised. This constant shifting of the substance of the subject would be understandable if there were no perspective to suggest a more appropriate norm. But as with any liberal art, there is no other place to look for the relatively abiding substance of its nature than in notable works that are hallmarks of its history.

The study of mathematics will not necessarily develop intellectual rigor and imaginative power as general properties of the mind, but the writings of first-rate mathematicians exemplify these qualities. "To appreciate the living spirit rather than the dry bones of mathematics," remarks E. E. Bell, "it is necessary to inspect the work of a master at first hand....The very crudities of the first attack on a significant problem by a master are more illuminating than all the pretty elegance of the standard texts which has been won at the cost of perhaps centuries of finicky polishing." The nineteenth century mathematician N. H. Abel, when asked how in a brief six or seven years he managed to contribute so much to mathematics replied: "By studying the masters, not their pupils."

In an address to the London branch of the Mathematical Association, Whitehead declared:

> "The end of all grammatical studies of the student in classics is to read Virgil and Horace — the greatest thought of the greatest men. Are we content, when pleading for the adequate representation in education of our own science to say that the end of a mathematical training is that the student should know the properties of the nine-point circle? I ask you frankly, is it not rather a 'come-down'...? Euclid's fifth book is regarded by those qualified to judge as one of the triumphs of Greek mathematics....Nothing can be more characteristic of the hopelessly illiberal character of the traditional mathematical education that the fact that this book has always been omitted. It deals with ideas, and therefore was ostracized."

In devising a mathematics curriculum for elementary liberal education, we must ask: (1) Which are the first-rate works that might be appropriate to each stage of learning? (2) How can these be taught best — i.e., both in relating to their own excellence and to the other parts of the mathematics curriculum? (3) What preliminary instruction, if any, would be necessary in order to learn to read these works?

Arithmetic paves the way for the study of algebra, which is the extension of arithmetic by other means. In this first preparatory part of the mathematics curriculum, the young student gains the initial experience with the language out of which concepts, structure, and analysis can develop. He comes upon structure after the mathematical edifice has been lived in for a while.

Timing is of the essence in education. Children should be introduced to the language of mathematics similarly to the way they are taught a modern foreign language — learning its patterns of thought and manner of expression by getting the hang of how it works in practice.

In the Old Dispensation, arithmetic was made dubious by the value it was deemed to have in daily life, and tedious by being divorced from its history and conceptual foundation. Arithmetic has a practical value that must not be neglected (as indeed the New Math did neglect it); but even more significantly, it is a gateway to the study of mathematics as a liberal art.

The abstract nature of the language should be trusted from the beginning. Teaching arithmetic with rods and blocks or in reference to social activities, like an imaginary trip to the zoo (if there are 12 monkeys in the orange cage and eight disappear, how many are left?), make the mistake of using physical "realia" and anecdotal material for mathematical reality — as if, like Antaeus, the mind needed to keep at least one foot on the ground in order to think mathematically. The mind is born and bred in signs and symbols. Out of the nettle, abstraction, mathematical meaning is plucked.

A thorough grounding in arithmetic should be given in the first six grades. The seventh grade might be used as a water-shed year in which various mathematical interests could be cultivated: the application of mathematics to music, mathematical puzzles and games, and the reading of essays on mathematical thinking (e.g., W. K. Clifford's "The Exactness of Mathematical Laws" and J. W. N. Sullivan's "Mathematics As an Art")*

The Seventh Grade would also be an appropriate time for the study of mathematical notation. In no other science or art, with the possible exception of music, does the development of the means of expression coincide with the development of the thought to the extent that it does in mathematics. "Half the battle in mathematics," said Laplace, "is the invention of a good notation."

The signs of zero, equal, infinity, are landmarks of intellectual history. The study of mathematical signs, selected on the basis of their influence, their contemporary relevance, their relation to other signs in the mathematical galaxy, their appropriateness to elementary education, their importance as ideas — in short, according to criteria similar to those by which the entire program is devised — would not only give much needed historical perspective to the study of mathematics but would at the same time deepen the understanding of its nature.

Mathematics didn't come into being, once and for all, at some remote golden age, and ought not be studied as if it did. Not all mathematical ideas are of equal importance, but one gains no inkling from school mathematics of the basic fact that in mathematics, as in life, there are trivial as well as momentuous ideas. This fact would be more likely to manifest itself if the development of mathematical thought were evidenced more clearly.

---

*For sources of material in the literature of mathematics, see James R. Newman (ed.) *The World of Mathematics*, 4 vols. (New York: Simon and Schuster, 1956)

In the study of mathematics as a liberal art, first-rate mathematics would be brought into the curriculum at the first opportunity. Given the nature of mathematics and given the nature of the human mind, the student will have developed the intellectual maturity to learn to read a few of the works of mathematical genius by the time that he comes to the last three years of his elementary education — the eighth, ninth, and tenth grades. In these three years not a great deal of original mathematics can be read, but at least a genuine beginning can be made. All that elementary education can do at its best is to made a good beginning.

One possible plan for these three years would be an intensive study of geometry. "Whenever I went far enough," said the noted British mathematician J. J. Sylvester, "into any mathematical question, I found I touched, at last, a geometrical bottom." And Scott Buchanan remarks (in *Poetry and Mathematics*): "The first and perhaps the most illuminating question in mathematics is, what is a geometrical figure?"

The first place in the conventional school mathematics program that the subject begins to take on intellectual excitement for most students is when it comes to Euclid. Geometry is the one experience with mathematics that the average student (the one with the "non-mathematical mind") enjoys; and, interestingly enough, this is where he first comes to the study of mathematics as a liberal art.

That he has had the intellectual pleasure of understanding geometrical proofs will prove important to his education whether or not he ever has occasion to use geometry for any other purpose. Moreover, the influence of Euclid in the history of culture is a fact of considerable significance.

"It might well be asked," wrote Solomon Bochner, "What is the explanation of the fact that Euclid's *Elements* has played such a vigorous part for more than two millenia in the intellectual life of the West? This despite the fact that Euclid's work ought to have been any educationist's nightmare....It never offers any 'motivation', it has no illuminating 'asides', it does not attempt to make anything 'intuitive', and it avoids 'applications' to a fault....

"But it nevertheless survived intact all the turmoils, ravages, and illiteracies of the dissolving Roman Empire, of the early Dark Ages, of the Crusades and of the plagues and famines of the later Middle Ages.

"And it is astonishing that in the America of 1860 a consummate grassroots politician of the then Mid-Western Frontier should have thought that adding to a mixture of log cabin and railsplitting a six books worth of Euclid would make the mixture more palatable to an electorate across the country."

The first great innovation in geometric thinking following the geometry of the Greeks came in the seventeenth century with Descartes' invention of analytic geometry. This achievement exerted tremendous influence on the subsequent development of mathematical thought. There is a clear, logical progression from arithmetic to algebra to Euclidean geometry to analytic geometry that would richly satisfy the intellectual and esthetic possibilities of the mathematics curriculum in elementary liberal education, up to and including the tenth grade.

What is characteristically powerful of an art presents the best case for studying it. Despite the fact that at least occasional allusions to its beauty are *de rigueur* in teaching mathematics (like an uncertain lover who must constantly reassure himself as to the worth of his beloved), this quality may seem frail indeed to serve as a primary reason for teaching it in school. Nevertheless, it is a reason that commends the study of mathematics as good in itself, which is more plausible than as a possible career happening in the distant future.

The satisfaction to be derived from the esthetics aspect of mathematics "ought not to be refused to learners capable of enjoying it," wrote Bertrand Russell, "for it is of a kind to increase our respect for human power and our knowledge of the beauties belonging to the abstract world."

In the school years of the student's life, he is likely to find mathematical beauty and elegance a more congenial kind of meaning than that stated by a School handbook: "Mathematics is a tool for competent living."

Professors of other subjects in the humanities are inclined to be somewhat skeptical of the notion of mathematical beauty and to suppose that this view is advanced as a kind of ruse to enable mathematicians to climb upon the *humanitas* bandwagon. *In Science: the Glorious Entertainment*, Jacques Barzun dismisses Russell's defense of beauty in mathematics as "sheer affectation" and "nonsense." Mr. Barzun lumps mathematics and science together and declares that both "lack the sensual element that is indispensable to art. Something to see, hear, touch, and mouth over...." In the same book he has previously stated: "Fact and truth embody emotion as well as thought. This is what Pascal meant when he said that the proposition in geometry could become a sentiment. " (This "fact and truth" confuse the issue a step further. Most contemporary mathematicians would describe the nature of pure mathematics without recourse to either term.)

It is a necessity of the mind to find order in things — from the motion of the heart to the motion of the heavens, in things real and in things imaginary — and, finding it, to find it pleasing. And it is more than merely "the sensual element" that we are able to "see."

The discovery of a tolerable order anywhere in the universe helps dispel the loneliness of existence. It argues for a compatibility between the structure of the universe and the structure of the mind. Where a model of order is expressed with such economy and power of thought as may be found in the best mathematics, it is not astonishing that being seen, it should also be found pleasing.

"Beauty," wrote G. H. Hardy, "is the first test: there is no permanent place in the world for ugly mathematics....The best mathematics is *serious* as well as beautiful....The 'seriousness' of a mathematical theorem lies, not in its practical consequences, which are usually negligible, but in the *significance* of the mathematical ideas which it connects...."

"The beauty of a mathematical theorem *depends* a great deal on its seriousness, as even in poetry the beauty of a line may depend to some extent on the significance of the ideas which it contains. The ideas do matter to the pattern, even in poetry, and much more naturally, in mathematics...." [Italics his]

Although Hardy doesn't say specifically what he means by the "seriousness" or "significance" of mathematical ideas (in addition to their esthetic interest), it would appear, since he excludes "practical consequences," that he means " even in poetry" mathematical ideas are also distinguished (and distinguishable from each other) by their intellectual and imaginative specific gravity.

But the practical consequences of mathematical beauty may not be altogether as remote as Hardy suggests, and may connote a utilitarian as well as an esthetic sentiment. "It is more important to have beauty in one's equations," writes P. A. M. Dirac, who shared with Schrödinger the 1933 Nobel Prize in physics, "than to have them fit experiment....If one is working from the point of view of getting beauty in one's equations, and if one has really sound insight, one is on a sure line of progress."

In a liberal arts curriculum, teaching mathematics solely for its practical use is the most impractical way to teach it. It cannot be done this way without corrupting the nature of the art and discouraging its further study. Mathematics is as able as music, poetry, or visual art, to generate its own power of attraction.

The mind wants to know and to remember nothing so much as what is pleasing to it. Why should this not apply as well to the beauty of mathematics as to any other liberal art?

Problems arise in the course of learning to read mathematics, as they arise in the course of learning to read poetry and drama. But it is pedantry and intellectual death to try to relate every mathematical idea to its applications. "Some of the greatest mathematical discoveries," wrote Scott Buchanan, "by the greatest mathematical minds have been theorems that they could not prove; some have never been proved. The fact of the matter is that anything worth discovering in mathematics does not need proof; it needs only to be seen or understood." If first-rate mathematics creates patterns that are richly significant and even beautiful, then learning to read it in works of this quality justifies itself for the same reasons as learning any liberal art.

A good education should teach the student to read in more ways than one: a work of poetry by the numbers; a work of mathematics, poetically.

Here, too, is the kind of learning that is characteristically liberal. Mathematics has its own ways of telling the extravagance and joy and play that are possible at the periphery when there is confidence that the center holds.

Chapter VIII
THE DEVELOPMENT OF MUSICAL INTELLIGENCE

The student should be guided to think of music in the way the finest musicians do.
Within the limitations of his skills — and to the highest degree practical —
the student then operates on all fronts as if he were a totally experienced,
all-around musician. The child should experience, in microcosm, all
the pre-occupations of a professional musician. He should expect
his rhythm to be accurate, his conducting beat firm, his
tone clearly produced. Everything must be
done honestly, well, and with flair.

Music In Our Schools: Report
on the Yale Seminar of Music Education

E ducation has to do with the meaning of things. But what is the meaning of music beyond that of being either a phenomenon of sound explicable in terms of physical laws and quantitative measurement or a simple sensuous pleasure? How is the study of music justified in liberal education?

The names of composers are enshrined, along with other great artists, in recognition of the significance of their achievement. But in what does music's significance consist? What is the exact nature of the meaning upon which depends the value of music to education?

"The precise meaning of music," writes Aaron Copland, "is a question that should never have been asked." But then he goes on to say: "Anyone can tell the difference between a sad piece and a joyous one. The talented listener recognizes not merely the joyous quality of the piece, but also the specific shade of joyousness— whether it be troubled joy, delicate joy, carefree joy, hysterical joy, and so forth." And he then concludes that: "Next to fathoming the meaning of music, I find this point [structural understanding] the most obscure in our understanding of the auditory faculty."

Music was included in the *quadrivium* because of its relation to mathematics. This meaning of music can be seen insofar as "its form may be reduced to perfectly definite rules expressed in numbers, from which it cannot free itself without entirely ceasing to be music."(Schopenhauer)

But although musical form may be "reduced" to mathematics, its meaning is not characteristically known in this way. Ratios and proportions that are to be found in music do not resolve the dilemma of its meaning. It is in its "sounding reality" that the central meaning of music must be found.

Furthermore, how can the arrangement of notes on a musical scale and their performance as musical tones have not only meaning but serious, weighted meaning? "In speaking of musical compositions," wrote Eduard Hanslick, the nineteenth century music critic, "...a critical mind easily distinguishes real thoughts from hollow phrases, precisely as in speech."

It is the "real thoughts" of a musical composition that constitute its specific gravity. But what is there in a musical work that enables a critical mind to make this distinction? How do musical tones in combination communicate this intelligence? Whence comes the difference in one weight of meaning and another between two musical works? What is there in the music itself that compels the acknowledgement, not only of musical meaning but, of a meaning that has artistic and musical power?

These questions have peculiar, pressing, and poignant relevance to the study of a discipline whose meaning is subject to such radical doubt.

Music is often referred to as a kaleidoscope of sound. But we don't usually think one kaleidoscope capable of more serious meaning than another. One model may have a greater number of colored pieces than another, or a greater variety of colors and shapes represented, or more mirrors to allow for a larger number of combinations. But of what intellectual or esthetic import are these differences? What weight of meaning do they imply? How should we take one kaleidoscope more seriously than another?

Allowing for auditory and cultural differences, listeners to the same work will in general all hear it as intelligible sound; to be enjoyed or not, to be moved by it or not, but at least to recognize it for what it is: namely, music.

The kind of sound that music makes rational is musical sound; a tautology, to be sure, but how else is it possible to say that the reason for recognizing music as music is that it is, or may rightly be understood as — music?

The musical meaning that is heard simply because music is distinguished from mere noise is sufficient to account for the fact that there are different responses to and varying degrees of appreciation for what is heard. One listener, for whatever reason, may like one kind of music and another listener a different kind. This fact presents no great problem of understanding. But how music can "rationalize" sound in ways that not only signify serious thoughts (as opposed to hollow or superifical ones), as well as the precise meaning of these thoughts, surely does present a problem.

The language of music is the most paradoxical of the major languages of human communication. It is at once a young art (music notation as we know it is less than three hundred years old) and an ancient, pre-historic one; a Western art ("The one cultural frontier which precisely defines Europe," writes the historian A.J. P. Taylor, "is the major and minor diatonic scale....") and a universal one; it is both precise and protean, abstract and concrete.

The essence of music, wrote Hanslick, is "sound in motion." More particularly, it is the *dramatization* of sound in motion: any motion, hence music's "universal" sound; one particular motion, hence its sensuous sound.

Music, like mathematics, occupies two realms of meaning simultaneously. Its purely musical meaning finds validity simply by means of musical tones in their sounding relations. Its extra-musical meaning, which is as bound to the musical as the partials to the fundamental, achieves its validity by analogy and association.

To the meaning that is achieved in music by the development of a musical idea, no analogy need apply. This is music's genetic meaning, so to speak, which is what is heard in sensuous and intelligible immediacy. "The finale comes like a fulfillment after much premonition and desire, whereas the same event, unprepared for, might hardly have been observed. The whole technique of music is but an immense elaboration of this principle. It deploys a sensuous harmony by a sort of dialectic, suspending and resolving it, so that the parts become distinct and their relation vital." (Santayana)

The music achieves its significance in this respect by musical tones coherently related and developed to their musically consistent resolution. The theme establishes a premise, as it were, upon which the work is built. It achieves the significance of its form by the tones of the work being related to this theme and to each other in terms that are musically rational or, less redundantly, simply musical.

But the meaning of music is hardly exhausted by the interest we find in one pattern of sound changing into another. A single musical tone becomes music in combination with other musical tones. As these tones have no denotative meaning, it is to their connotations that we must look if we would find the meaning other than its own sound that music calls into being.

In Suzanne Langer's inquiry into the meaning of music (*Feeling and Form*), which continues and expands the esthetic adumbrated in an earlier work (*Philosophy in a New Key*), she comes to the conclusion that "music is not a kind of language." The reason that she adduces for this opinion is that music is lacking in the kind of meaning that is "always explicable, definable, and translatable."

In any sense taken from the language of speech, the extra-musical meaning is bound to seem fugitive, ambiguous, unconvincing, guesswork. Whenever the meaning in one language is determined by criteria taken from another, it is to be expected that it will be found either incongruent or non-existent. Although it is true that extra-musical meaning is always inexplicable, indefinable, and untranslatable, its meaning beyond that of merely formal import is acknowledged even by those most concerned to guard the integrity of the purely musical sound.

In The *Beautiful in Music*, for example, Hanslick writes: "The beauty of composition is specifically musical...i.e., it inheres in the combination of musical sounds and is independent of all alien extramusical notions." He concedes, however, the analogy "between action in space and action in time; between the color, texture, and size of an object and the pitch, timbre, and strength of a tone; and it is for this reason quite practicable to paint an object musically. The pretension, however, to describe by musical means the 'feeling' which the falling snow, the crowing cock, or a flash of lighning excites in us is simply ludicrous."

Although Hanslick is rigorous in his determination to exclude as much of extra-musical meaning as possible, he is obliged to leave the door slightly ajar. "It is," he says, "aesthetically, quite correct to speak of a theme as having a sad or noble accent, but not as expressing the sad or noble feelings of the composer."

This is cutting the matter fairly thin. If a theme can have sad or noble accents, why should these not be understood as expressing the sad or noble feelings of the composer — not necessarily as he feels them at the moment of composition (although why not then also?), but as he has felt and is able to recollect them? Once the principle of analogy is admitted to musical meaning, it is difficult to exclude it altogether from application to whatever phenomena have, or like feelings may be imagined to have, motion.

There is no clear distinction that can be made in music between the purely subjective and purely objective, the particular and the universal, the denotative and the connotative.

Music is a universal language not least because the associations made by its sounding reality establish similar associations between different individuals and different cultures, as well as dissimilar ones.

In *Swann's Way* Proust writes of Swann: "He knew...that the field open to the musician is not a miserable stave of seven notes, but an immeasurable keyboard (still, almost all of it, unknown), here and there only, separated by the gross darkness of its unexplored tracts, some few among the millions of keys, keys of tenderness, of passion, of courage, of serenity, which compose it, each one differing from all the rest as one universe differs from another, have been discovered by certain great artists...showing us what richness, what variety lies hidden, unknown to us, in that great black impenetrable night...."

What are several of the conditions that are generally considered to qualify music as a language? One, the invention of music notation and of music instruments; two, music literature and music history; three, the development of music theory as a kind of logic in sound that argues harmony, melody, and rhythm as ideal possibilities. But, historically, music antedates music notation, music literature, music instruments, and music theory.

The way in which music directs the mind of the listener now toward this association of tones and now toward that suggests dramatic issues and interests that inhere in these associations.

Music expands the meaning that we hear in the correlation between spirit and sound; between, for example, anger's taut vibrancy or despair's low resonance in the human voice.

Music expresses extra-musical meaning primarily in ways that are subjective; that is, the connection with external reality is unmistakably made, but there can be no "correct" verifiable interpretation of this meaning; it is not explicit. "Nor is music the only idle cerebral commotion that enlists attention and presents issues no less momentous for being quite imaginary; dreams do the same....Music has its own substitute for conceptual distinctness....Music creates a new realm of form...."(Santayana)

Music and dreams both communicate a sense of the reality of a drama the exact meaning of which is only intimated. In listening to music, as in a dream, we recognize, however indirectly or indistinctly, the pure, deep, subtle, extensive presence of meaning by the way in which the work invests, shapes, cultivates, bestows, turns toward, turns from — its own reality.

We listen to music as a "co-rational" (St. Augustine) phenomenon. Although music may suggest whatever aspects of existence coincide in the listener's mind with changes in the pitch, volume, timbre, and duration of musical tones, it cannot explicitly depict any image, express any feeling, define any idea, or describe any event, except by so transforming these into its own substance of purely musical meaning that whatever else remains translatable into another language is so much the worse for the music.

Although the language of music cannot precisely identify anything outside itself (Onomatopoeia is either a trivial or only an apparent exception), it can, by analogy and suggestion, find powerful correspondences in the human mind, "Even the purest phenomenon in the natural world of sound," writes Hanslick, "— the sound of birds — has no relation to music, as it cannot be reduced to our scale....The 'music' of nature and the music of man belong to two distinct categories....Not the voices of animals but their gut is of importance to us; and the animal to which music is most indebted is not the nightingale but the sheep."

Composer, performer, and listener are together engaged in sharing a communication that, on one level, they hear in the same way; and, on another level, each hears as it is filtered through his own memory and imagination. Like a touch or glance, the meaning of music is direct, instant, universal — and ambiguous.

Music appears to demonstrate a meaning that is denotative when words and music coincide closely with each other, as in title, program, and song; when the words as a veritable Adam identify the musical tones. However, words of different and even opposite meaning may fit equally well the same musical pattern. Moreover, when words and music have no inherent affinity for each other, the meaning of each is confused — or heightened by contrast.

While the music itself cannot express a denotative meaning, it can, in association with words, suggest an extension or deepening of meaning. The words bear the denotation that is in turn supported by connotation in the musical tones.

In *Don Giovanni*, for example, the libretto gives the dramatic quality of the music a tragic dimension — the sensuousness falls into sensuality as a form of the spirit's lust to dominate — that the tones alone could not. Or, to take a corollary example from the same work: the chilling mutuality of words and music when the statue of the Commendatore stands at the entrance to the banquet hall and in four, slow, grave accents tolls the name of Don Giovanni. The tones of the voice of eternity summoning the sinner to repentance effect an emotional response in the listener that the words alone could not.

As pure geometry is not about objects in space, but about the relation of certain mathematical ideas to each other; so Beethoven's C-sharp Minor Sonata, Opus 27, No. 2, is not "about" the appearance of moonlight on water, but about the harmony, melody, and rhythm of its tones in particular musical arrangement.

In one sense of its meaning, music stands in contrast to pure mathematics, insofar as it has its identity in immediate sensuous perception; and, in another, stands with it, insofar as the meaning of this identity is undetermined by any empiric connection.

But while mathematics is none the worse for its empiric association, a "program" is often more a distraction from the music than an aid to hearing and understanding it for what it is.

Although the meaning of neither music nor mathematics is secured by external factors of coincidence, both are capable of indirectly affecting a reality other than their own. Mathematical invention may lead to scientific discovery; music may, and often does, not only suggest emotion but affect it.

Both the historical event and the musical work illustrate the relation of human act to human freedom. But unlike the events of historical time, the musical state is based on a premised time and a feigned motion. Music, writes Kierkegaard, "cannot express the historical in the temporal process."

We hear a "lingering" or a "skipping" in a musical phrase; but these are terms imputed to the music, not expressed by it. Tones are loud or soft, short or long, "high" or "low" relative to each other in the context given. Musical texture is pure form. The tones of music, built out of frequency vibrations and transmitted by the compression of air, are as "real" as bricks. But in the pattern of sounds made out of them, the tones neither linger, nor skip, nor perform any other denotatively descriptive movement. Musical patterns are virtualities, the stuff of dreams, positing another kind than historical reality.

Music, dreams, and pure mathematics have a meaning that we take seriously, despite the fact that they do not *explicitly* describe or define a reality extrinsic to their own.

The language of music doesn't grow and develop apart from its literature, as does the language of words; it has no empiric base, as does mathematics; it has no representational base, as does visual art. Nevertheless, music does not wholly determine its own identity. Because the listener's mind is the place where the music is encountered, it is heard as both life and music have combined in him. There is no more an innocent ear in music than an innocent eye in visual art. We cannot posit ourselves back in the Garden without the insinuation of post-Garden tremors; the historical inevitably intrudes. It is in the mingling of the historical with the musical consciousness that extra-musical meaning is heard.

Despite the quandary presented by the problem of the meaning of music, it would be a rash judgment that found no place in education for so powerful a form of expression.

According to the strict logic of the case, it may be that the sounding reality of meaning in music is too ambiguous. Perhaps it is only esthetic bias prompting the conviction that what we can learn from music is essential to an education worthy of being called liberal.

Be that is it may, if we had to choose, in constructing a program of education for Everychild, between the strict logic on the one hand and the music on the other, we should prefer to be inconsistent. That it isn't by logic alone but by experience also that education practices its art, let the presence of music be heard as witness.

Music does not compete seriously for a conspicuous place on the present School scene, but few appear disturbed by this state of affairs, or view with concern the lack of opportunity for children in American schools to acquire a decent music education.

No one would be well advised to try to excite public alarm by a book on why Johnny can't sing.

Criticism of music education in the schools is conspicuously missing from the continuing public debate on education. Despite State-of-the-Art Electronic Equipment and All That, the assertion that music is as important a part of elementary education as science or mathematics would in all probability be taken generally as an expression of whimsy if not a symptom of softmindedness.

Music drains no marshes, launches no satellites, wins no wars. It is important only because its language finds significant resonance in the human spirit.

We do not know how or to what extent intelligence may be inherited, but there is no mystery at all to how it may otherwise be acquired. The aim of music education is to cultivate musical intelligence. Wasting the intelligence of Everychild is particularly objectionable where, as in music, his potentialities are clearly less disadvantaged by other factors than by lack of educational opportunity.

The School affliction that evidences itself in every other sector of the curriculum spares the musical and visual arts least. Music education in the schools today is largely counterfeit or largely absent. Serious musical standards do not apply. The "rhythm-fun-for-little-folks" approach cuts the heart out of the rhythm and poisons the fun.

"Of all branches of music education," declares the *Harvard Dictionary of Music*, " that connected with the public schools is the most static and reactionary....But the American is no less innately musical than members of other races....It follows, therefore, that the greatest need is a teaching body that is better educated musically...."

It won't ever be possible to establish a successful alliance between School authorities and serious musicians if the latter are forced into a subordinate role in matters of musicianship. Not the loosely educated School teacher but the serious musician — taught by the best traditions of his art and imbued with the passion of transmitting them authentically — must be the one to whom the schools look for guidance and leadership in developing a serious music curriculum.

There is no question that the fundamentals of a sound music education can and should be given to all children. "The question is," said Humpty Dumpty, "which is to be master — that's all." If a real music education is to be given school students, then it must be real musicians who give it to them. There isn't a chance of Everychild getting this kind of music education in the schools unless the same musical standards apply there as in the real world of music.

How seriously do we want to educate Everychild?

We ought to want to educate him as well as we can. In the plan proposed here for his music education, there is nothing proposed that would be beyond his musical capability. The study of music is important enough to warrant providing him with daily musical instruction as a major part of his elementary education.

The first aim of teaching music as a liberal art is musicianship — the art by which music is heard, composed, and performed; the quality of response to musical ideas; the essential measure of musical art.

The entire music curriculum from beginning to end should be one, ten-year, unified program in the fundamentals of musicianship.

Secondly, a proper music education would acquaint Everychild with a representative selection of musical masterworks, at least a few of which he will study closely and in depth. "The central works should be chosen," says the Report of the Yale Seminar on Music Education, "not because they are among those 'that every high school graduate should know', but rather, on the strength of what might be called maximum resonance; that is, their capacity to motivate the student to seek further experience and understanding."

This principle of "maximum resonance" has obvious application to and implication for every part of a liberal arts program. The central works in all the arts are those that possess the most power to motivate the student to want more of the same, and that lead him to the heart of the language. Studying the music of Bach or Mozart or Beethoven is not simply learning "technique," but learning to understand and enjoy the meaning of music where it is most meaningful.

It is primarily the music that educates the student — and it had better be good.

The point would hardly seem to need belaboring (except for the fact of current School practice) that, more than any other factor, the quality of the music justifies its study and anchors the quality of music education.

"The repertory used in most school systems in the United States," says the Yale Report, "...is corrupted by arrangements, touched-up editions, erroneous transcriptions, and tasteless parodies to such an extent that authentic work is rare....To the extent that artificial music is taught to children, to that extent are they invited to hate it."

In a first-rate music education the works of great composers would not suffer the fate of either being cast to outer darkness or of being made known only cheaply and superficially. A serious music education would explore as many ways as possible of bringing to the listening consciousness of the student the best of musical art.

Thirdly, a music education of this quality would provide the student with the opportunity, and possibly even the ability, to perform music well. He needs the experience of listening to music in a way that engages his maximum interest and at the same time brings him into serious communication with musical ideas. The most direct and most effective way to accomplish this is by teaching him to be a performer.

From the First Grade on he must be encouraged to think of learning to play music as an intrinsic part of his life — acquiring competence in, hence responsibility toward, the discipline required for the proper performance of good music.

The minute and seemingly trivial difference in playing the tones of a musical piece with one emphasis rather than another reflects, as a performer knows better than a non-performer, a world of meaning. Writing of the importance of music to education, Aristotle asks: "Why should we learn ouselves? Why cannot we attain true pleasure and form a correct judgment from hearing others, like the Lacedaemonians? For they, without learning music, nevertheless can correctly judge, as they say, of good and bad melodies." But, he continues, "It is difficult, if not impossible, for those who do not perform to be good judges of the performance of others....We conclude, then, that they [children] should be taught music in such a way as to become not only critics but performers."

It is in active response to music that the student should begin and continue with his studies. Every child is a performer from the first day that he learns to sing in tune, to beat a drum in rhythm, or to dance in unison to another's beat. He begins as music itself began.

Giving piano instruction to all children enrolled in our schools might be considered a formidable undertaking; but a nation that prides itself on its practical ability and its desire to provide the best possible education for every child ought not be daunted by the prospect.

Group piano instruction offers a feasible way for this to be done. "In the past quarter of a century," writes Marilyn K. Davis in the *Music Educator's Journal*, "a quiet revolution has been in progress in the piano teaching professsion — the gradual displacement of the private lesson in favor of group instruction....Experiments by music educators throughout the nation have proven beyond doubt that musical instruction given in a group situation succeeds to a far greater degree in fostering interest and producing results than does the private lesson."

Perhaps the idea of teaching all children to play the piano as part of their elementary education is visionary. But what is vision — educational or otherwise — without a touch of the quixotic?

If virtually every family in the United States can afford to own a television set, it is not unthinkable that a musical instrument might be found there also. Let the child be a performer in life, not just a passive observer.

The purpose of teaching the school student to perform music is to further his understanding of music, his love of music, his life-long pleasure from music.

In a ten-year music curriculum, the student could learn to play, in addition to the piano, other types of musical instruments— percussion, wind, string. He should be taught on instruments of good quality. If we demand nothing but the best for our military hardware, we should be able to afford the same standard for the education of our children.

Fourthly, music education in the schools should teach Everychild how music "rationalizes" sound. There is no part of the following college course description that coud not apply in a ten-year curriculum to the teaching of music theory in the schools also. "The work of the tutorial includes an investigation of rhythm in words as well as in notes, a thorough investigation of the diatonic system, a study of the ratios of musical interludes, and a consideration of melody, counterpoint, and harmony. None of these is done apart from the sounding reality of good music.

"Seminars on great works of music are included as part of the regular seminar schedule. Instead of reading a text, students listen to recordings of a composition and familiarize themselves with its score before the seminar meets. Group discussion of a work of music, as of a book, facilitates and enriches the understanding of it." (*Catalog*, St. John's College, Annapolis, MD, and Santa Fe, NM)

Music found its place in the *quadrivium* — along with the strange bedfellows of arithmetic, geometry, and astronomy — because antiquity and the middle ages viewed it primarily as an art of good measurement. But because music occurs in immediacy, the arts of reflection, measurement, and analysis must be subordinate to hearing the music in fuller awareness. "Reflection destroys the immediate," writes Kierkegaard, "and hence it is impossible to express the musical in language [i.e., of words]; but this apparent poverty of language is precisely its wealth."

That the music be listened to well is a pre-requisite to hearing its full resonance of meaning at any level — which is not to minimize its "rationality," but to emphasize that the mind is primarily engaged in the music according to the quality of attention given in listening to it in "immediacy."

The relationship between the art of good measurement and the art of good listening is clearly an intimate one. "And even things without life giving sound, whether pipe or harp, except they give a distinction in the sounds, how shall it be known what is piped or harped?" (*The Bible*: I Cor.14:7)

The development of the notation enabled the composer's ideas to become clearer and gave a distinction to the sounds, which in turn enabled the notation to be improved. Beethoven's insistence that his music be played according to his metronomic markings rather than the imprecise verbal indication of tempi by Italian words reflected his determination that the performance of the music express, as nearly as possible, his intentions and not the conductor's. (But in performance "nearly as possible" obviously means in effect that the interpretation of the music is determined in the mind not only of the composer, but of the conductor and the performers also.)

The development of the notation — and such technical innovations as the metronome and the improvement of instrument making— effected a shift in authority from the conductor or performer to the composer, and in doing so made the meaning of the language more precise, and therefore more powerful.

Letting the mind wander, upstairs and downstairs and into my lady's chamber, may be a descriptive but cannot be argued as a normative way of listening to music. All musical activities converge at the point of listening. Analyses of or analogies to musical sound must give precedent to the act of listening, which is an achievement not cultivated in an intellectual or esthetic vacuum, but by the various disciplines of musical art, including the understanding of its rational foundations.

Discussing his own musical education, Paul Hindemith writes: "Singing was the foundation of all musical work....The practical knowledge of more or less all instruments was a *sine qua non*....Hand in hand with this daily all-round routine in instrumental training went a solid instruction in the theory of music...."

In the singing voice, the listening to music, the playing of several different instruments, the study of music theory — here is a solid basis upon which a sound music education might, if we were serious about it, be given Everychild.

Finally, the music curriculum in the schools should introduce Everychild to types of music outside the classical repertory, including ethno-music, non-Western music, jazz, folk, popular, country-Western, and experimental music. He should learn to listen, as a liberal artist in the making, to all kinds of music, not so much as a separate exercise, but as an intrinsic part of his other musical activities.

Whether or not Plato's dictum that children should be taught music, "in order that they may learn to be more gentle, and harmonious, and rhythmical, and so more fitted for speech and action" is a valid theory of child psychology, it is as true today as in antiquity, that a child who grows up in ignorance of music has been deprived of a significant part of his education.

As we assume, or should assume, that Everychild will be a reader all his life if, from the beginning of his education, he is taught reading well; so too, it is not unreasonable to suppose that he will be a performer and lover of music all his life if, as a child, he is taught music well.

Chapter IX
THE LANGUAGE OF VISION AND THE VISION OF ART

I know of no art which calls for the use of more *intelligence* than drawing.
Whether it be a question of conjuring from the whole complex of
which is seen, the one pencil stroke that is right, of summarizing
a structure...every mental faculty finds its function in the task,
which no less forcibly reveals whatever personality
the artist may have. [Emphasis his]

Paul Valéry

Visual art is a manifesto declaring that life has a certain value and deserves
a certain quality of response. Things die in our sight; visual art is an Easter
of man's creation. It is also a way that man has sought through the ages to propitiate
the gods (or praise God), defeat his enemy, make the rains come, exorcise demons
of pain and despair, bring luck in hunting, welcome the morning, and see the
appearance of things as they have not been seen before.

Visual art is a way of rejoicing in the visualness of things. That there should be
roundness! that scarlet is!

The visual artist makes visible reality more visible; his work admits a life at the
surface. Visually, we are sleepwalkers; the visual artist wakens our open eyes.
"Doctor. 'You see, her eyes are open.' Gentlemen. 'Aye, but their sense is shut.'"
(*Macbeth*)

How well do we ever see anything? To see is to interpret; and wisdom is to
suspect how little we really see of those things that really matter.

The visual artist must come to terms with the appearance of things, but only that
he may give his own account of the reality he sees in them. Truth may or may not
please on being seen. But it is more real than its appearances — except as it is also
the appearances.

Appearance is — and is not — part of what we mean by "reality". In one sense,
it is as "real" as any other part, simply because of and in its appearance. But when
we oppose or contrast appearance to reality, we mean to distinguish the deceptive,
superficial, trivial, or hollow, from a more significant view of things.

The greatest art is prophetic, revealing the inadequacy of the appearances with
which we are most comfortable. Reality in this sense is a matter of value. It is the

sense in which we understand every human being to make the wager absolute. (Ladies and gentlemen, place your lives!)

An artist seeks to achieve his aim by observing appearances — and expressing them otherwise. Observe he must or he will come ill-prepared to the trial at issue; his "feigning"(from Latin *fingere*, to form, shape, invent) will be empty. The ability of the artist to discern astutely and accurately simply what is in the appearance of things is the first, necessary step to his taking command.

Joyce Cary, who was trained as a painter in his youth, writes of his teacher: "This was his cry all the time: 'What's it mean?' He would point at a knee and say, 'Look at this piece of boiled macaroni. What's that mean there? Which leg is she standing on?' 'The left.' 'Then why don't you show the tension in the hamstring?' 'It's in the shadow.' 'What's that matter? You're not trying to be a camera. You're trying to tell us something...'"

And, again, from the same work (*Art and Reality*): "The setting of the eye, different in every person, the bulge of the cornea in the eyeball, according to the direction of the gaze, cannot be seized by the most acute observer without some knowledge of anatomy....If he does notice a detail, he doesn't know what it means, whether it is an idiosyncrasy in the model, a deformity, or a shape common to all eyes in that special position. And his drawings will show his ignorance, his indecision."

The artist must impose his own order on the appearances; be master in his own house; hang or cherish the universe in his own way. If he hasn't the courage or ability to premise radically different forms than nature and existing art present to him, what can he claim that is his own?

The work of visual art makes visible the forms that lie concealed in shapes of visibility. Every work of visual art raises anew the question, How shall this be looked at to be seen? The difference between "looked at" and "seen" points to the distinction art makes between the meaning of appearance and of reality. The artist seeks to distinguish the one from the other when he questions how he shall see what is "really" there. The appearances of art are valid according as they provide better or worse answers or conjectures to this question.

In her novel *Ehrengard*, Isak Dinesen describes the artist as a seducer. "For what does seduction mean but the ability to make, with infinite trouble, patience, and perseverance, the object upon which you concentrate your mind give forth, voluntarily and enraptured, its very core and essence? Aye, and to reach, in the process, a higher beauty than it could ever, under any other circumstances, have attained? I have seduced an old earthenware pot and two lemons into yielding their inmost being to me, to become mine and, at that same moment, to become phenomena of overwhelming loveliness and delight."

The heart yearns for more than just the flash of spirit; it wants the spirit as seen in the color and shape and line of particular appearances, each with its own tactile invitation.

Reality, which is distinguished from appearance, is distinguished also from the artist's own grasp. It is both a will-of-the-wisp to his understanding and the anvil upon which his understanding is shaped or shattered.

The visual artist wants the spectator to see in his work the validity that could not be seen, or not seen as well, except in and by means of its specific sensory representation.

If we choose to call the perception empowered in us by the work of visual art a seeing "beyond" appearance or "into" reality, there can be no objection to this as a figure of speech. But a work of art achieves distinction not by disparaging the significance of appearance, but by its power to reveal appearance significantly. Nothing is as it appears, but appearances signify everything that is.

What presumably, Bernard Berenson meant by the importance of the tactile in painting is the way in which the sense of touch and the sense of vision act in the imagination upon each other. The impulse to touch a work of visual art and to feel its texture is universal. We "touch" with our eyes and "see" with our touch, and we do both by virtue of appearance.

All that there is to look at in a work of visual art is there to be seen. However, that all that is there can be looked at and yet not seen is, to paraphrase the title of the Chirico painting, the melancholy and mystery of visual art.

The appearances of things shadow a deeper, more formidable, more unfathomable reality. Because visual art has of necessity to do with appearances, it has also to witness to the difference between appearance and reality. "Seems, madam! Nay, it is; I know not 'seems'....But I have that within which passes show."(*Hamlet*)

Art has nothing but "seems" to reveal what "is." The difference between these is — we must believe for sheer sanity's sake — not finally a delusion. The life of art exists by virtue of this difference.

Art bridges the distance between appearance and reality, but preserves also the integrity of the distance between them.

The work of visual art achieves its aim not because it is where reality is "grasped," as by a sign, but because it is a   translucent and powerful place of being.

In the serenity of a landscape, or its terror, or its serenity and terror together, the artist emphasizes a common ground as well as a distance between the potent appearance and its more potent reality. He makes the world more real to us by revealing new possibilities and dramatizing the conflict occasioned by their emergence. Art changes shape into form, a human figure into a landscape, features into a human face: like things made unlike in a drama of opposing forces, unlike things made like in a leap of imagination.

In art appearances compel us to them: we make do with reality. In life it is reality that is hard to come back from and appearances that are expedient.

Visual art has to do with representation as it uses things that have appearance to suggest and dramatize insights, interpretations, and values, which have not.

A painting "means" as much as it makes visible, which is rather more than "a plane surface covered with colors arranged in a certain order." A work of visual art is no more the mere arrangement of its visual pattern apart from its representational sense than the subject of a work of poetic art is the mere arrangement of its sound pattern apart from its syntactic sense.

Visual art is iconic by nature. Every work of visual art, as Picasso observed, is a figure of some kind. But not every figure enables the reality of things beyond itself to cross over into its own painting reality; to effect, in Buber's terms, "a meeting with the world." Not every figure achieves metaphoric power.

Visual art moves toward, not away from, the representation of things because that is where their ambiguities can be most powerfully dramatized.

Significant form is expressed in purely abstract as well as in representational works. But there is a difference in the kind of meaning that each makes possible.

Non-representational art is engrossed in the sphere of general instances. The play of the elements of visual form unrooted in the particular, recognizable, shapes of existence anchor its meaning. It kicks out from under itself the basis of the means for feigning, but remaining to support it is a meaning intrinsic to the formal relationships of color and line, shape and light.

Representational art, unlike pure abstraction, is a point of departure, not of arrival; it brings together the essential visual elements to state a meaning extrinsic to them.

Visual art has no inherent system of notation; it has no way of expressing extrinsic meaning symbolically — and at the same time ambiguously — except by representation. It does not of course cease to be art when it becomes non-representational, but it does cease to possess the power of expressing meaning extrinsic to its formal elements.

Why should extra-musical meaning be possible, but not non-objective extra-visual meaning? If there is any principle that applies here, one can only suppose it to be, that where the formal elements of language lack the capability of communicating denotative and extrinsic meaning, as in music, then association and analogy must take over if other than meaning external to itself is to be convincingly imputed. But where this capability clearly is not lacking, as in visual art, then the formal elements of the language can communicate only the meaning intrinsic to these elements.

It is no myth that the gaze of a child is innocent. Because of the innocence that gives his vision a positive force and because the language of vision has no notation that a child must learn before he can use it, his use of this language may often achieve striking results. Children express themselves more "artistically" in this language than in any other.

However, color, line, texture, shape, achieve artistic validity only as vision and art and craftsmanship compose them. The artist has learned — of the language and of himself — to express with a disciplined and developed power what he feels powerfully. The iconography of a Paul Klee may seem childlike, but a real child is not *like* a child: he is one. An artist may spend the better part of a lifetime discovering the visual forms that speak truly for him and powerfully to us.

Art education must keep the way open for the student to develop his own iconography, his own visual style and ideas; but, at the same time, teach him the language of vision well enough to be able to express himself intelligently, imaginatively, and authentically.

Giving him crayons and other art materials with which to scribble, dibble, dabble, and putter, along with an encouraging pat and a few reassuring words, as is current School practice, cannot even with the utmost charity be described as education in visual art.

The first aim of art education — beginning in First Grade and continuing throughout the entire, ten-year program of elementary education — should be to teach visual art as a quality of response to visual phenomena. It should be to develop visual intelligence and imagination: to teach the student to look, which is to observe; to see, which is to discern; and to make, which is to interpret and transform.

Secondly, art education should teach Everychild to perceive with the eyes of others — in the work of great artists — as well as within his own peculiar variation of feeling, thought, and retina. It should give the student knowledge of representative masterpieces of different periods and styles.

Each generation has the responsibility to encourage what is alive in its art — and to discourage what is not. But lacking knowledge of, and taking part in discussions about, the central works in which the integrity of the art is to be seen most clearly is like trying to tell this difference in the dark.

The student will learn better what is to be his own way of seeing visual form when he has first learned to look with an eye informed by the best. "The examples of the great masters," wrote Gerard Manley Hopkins, "are the soul of education." But he also observed that: "The effects of studying masterpieces is to make me admire and do otherwise."

Part of art education at the elementary level consists in learning how to "read" works of visual art and part in learning how to use the language of vision; not, however, as separate halves but as one integrated course.

Everychild should learn the language as a serious artist does. He will be able to establish his authority over the space that he stakes out for himself only by first acquiring power over his medium.

Thirdly, the art student should learn the making and doing of visual art in every way possible: crafts, drawing, painting, photography, sculpture. "Draw and draw," wrote Ben Shahn, " and paint and learn to work in many media: try lithography and aquatint and silk screen. Know all that you can about art, and by all means have opinions."

If everything is Fun Now, craftsmanship may seem quaint and the long way around. And if a rigorous approach to art education seems antiquated, this may be because, having lost the way, the schools no longer know where to look for the beginning.

The development of technique engenders the increase of power, not only in the history of an art but also in the history of an individual's training and education.

In the preceding chapters on each of the languages of learning, a particular area of emphasis is suggested as a means to focus and to deepen the teaching of this language; in music, piano study; in mathematics, geometry; in the language of words, poetry (fairy tales, imaginative literature; memorable, precise, and compact speech of any kind). In visual art, competence in drawing might be considered the area of "specialization" that would serve to center the enterprise.

Fourthly, art study in elementary education should teach the student an ability to make discriminate, rational judgments about the ways in which visual intelligence and imagination employ the basic elements of space, line, color, shape, light, position, texture, density, size, to achieve composition, tension, proportion, perspective, movement, rhythm, harmony, drama — in a word, artistry.

Although the language of vision — unlike the language of words, of music, of mathematics — has no notation and therefore no "code" that must be "broken" as part of acquiring competence in its use, it does suggest an analogy to one in its "conventional vocabulary of basic forms" — ways in which fundamental elements of the language in relation to visual reality, optical laws, psychological phenomena, and human experience, generate its possibilities.

Like the primary elements in music, those in visual art have an inherent power to influence and suggest association with emotional and other aspects of existence. "A drawing is, among other things," writes Howard Warshaw, a contemporary artist and teacher, " a visual analogue. It does not transcribe material facts but rather reveals observations and relationships. Like an X-ray, it shows us, not what was seen, but what otherwise would not be seen."

The teaching of art that sees it only as play takes the deeper pleasure out of it. Genuine art discovers incongruity between the self and the world and shoulders the consequence; it discovers congruity between the self and the world and celebrates it.

Visual art is as meaningful a discipline as mathematics. "It is true," wrote Le Corbusier and Ozenfant, "that plastic art has to direct itself more directly to the sense than pure mathematics. But there is no art worth having without this excitement of an intellectual order." It could only improve education to introduce some imaginative play into the study of mathematics and some intellectual discipline into the study of visual art.

Finally, art education should teach the student to look with an open, a liberal, eye upon new ways of seeing the world of appearance: the magnificent possibility of seeing the world anew.

If we have no satisfactory answer to the question, What is art?, how can we profess to know what art has ever been?

When Herbert Read declares that the Italian Alberto Burri "is a representative artist of my time! Precisely because he challenges the whole tradition of 'fine art' which has about as much relevance to the Age of Hiroshima as a jewelled sword: Precisely because he takes old sacks, charred plywood, metal scrap, any character- istic debris of our time, and from this waste defiantly creates the magic of a work of art." — what does this mean? What worth inheres in work "precisely because" the artist takes "characteristic debris" as his materials? If all is not art that litters, what is the principle by which one distinguishes artistic trash from non-artistic garbage?

When it became impossible to tell where the "avant garde" left off and free enterprise began, the term itself became an anachronism. The combined forces of an affluent society and a cultural revolution went to prove nothing so much as that Bohemia and Philistia are sisters under the skin — the New Jerusalem followed hard upon by *The Wall Street Journal*.

However, again, it is the enduring that the real artist and the real educator want. Time is also a way of prevailing. To become a ninety-day wonder in the art world is not to win a very large victory. Although market prices are one criterion of acceptance, they are not an esthetic one.

The artist is a radical by nature. What is more radical than a new, powerful way of seeing? But to be radical must mean more than Anything Goes at its zaniest; it must mean the proving of a credible alternative. Art looked at as a variant of Monopoly has only one rule: if it's In, it's Out. Once this relatively simple piece of intelligence has been mastered, what else is there for a player to do — if he is a serious artist, a bona fide radical and not a clown — but to forget the market game and get on with the search for meaning and truth? There is a place for inspired nonsense, but utter confusion can be ridiculous without amusing.

Let who will claim artistic validity for his art. He may be right. But let him be up against the independent, critical, informed judgment of those who have a mind to see and whose interest in seeing perceptively is, like the artist, invested in the search for artistic truth.

The liberal spirit that is able to recognize and value even the strangest, most radical and experimental art must be allied with the uncompromising spirit that is able to recognize — and reject — the artistically feckless, pretentious, and hollow.

It is as possible to give Everychild an elementary education in the language of visual art as it is in the other languages of liberal education. But it requires an educational system that is at least as serious in its intent as to employ serious artists as teachers. Even where school districts now employ "specialists in art," visual art is not taught seriously; and there is, typically, little time given to the subject. Consequently, little competence and understanding in art are transmitted there.

A unified, comprehensive, rational, school program of visual art does not exist in our public schools for Everychild today. School does not see visual art as a subject that has a deeply humanistic content, indispensable to education. School students may "take" art once a week for years, but they do not acquire even its rudiments there.

Aptitude is no more a pre-requisite for learning the language of vision than it is for learning any other languages of genuine education. If students were educated only according to their interests or aptitudes, most subjects would be excluded, as would most students. That, for whatever reasons, some children are more apt than others in general, and in some subjects in particular, is hardly to be disputed. But this piece of worldly wisdom is a place from which to start, not in which to stick.

The fact that a student can't draw a straight line need be no disabling condition in teaching him fundamentals of art. Insofar as art education is interested in straight lines, it can serve the purpose of stimulating the student's thought about them. Reflection about straight lines may lead him to thinking about lines that are curved. Eventually he may want to try thinking about lines that are straight looked at one way and curved looked at another: lines to engage him in revery.

Education should provide Everychild with the right stuff to daydream. If imagination is encouraged in him when he is young, it may one day help keep him from being buried prematurely.

The search for meaning that justifies the exertion of an adult's mind also justifies the validity of the child's endeavor. But the artistic maturity required in the making of a genuine work of art engages the mind too comprehensively than is possible for childhood. The child cannot see the appearances of the world in the way necessary to describe with an artist's understanding, suffering, imagination, conviction, strength — a brave new one.

The eye is a part of the brain; the "eye" is also a part of the mind. A child cannot see as an adult because he lacks the understanding that comes with experience. The life that the artist interprets and reveals in his work is a wonder of contrast, of miraculous escape, of death, of resurrection. He who has seen into the self's abyss has destruction, degradation, decay, against which life must be made to come alive. An adult may be surprised by joy; a child finds its absence incomprehensible. Much of the suffering of childhood is rooted in the simple inability to place experience in a context of understanding large and deep enough for the self's need.

"Though a child is often artistic," wrote André Malraux, "he is not an artist. For his gift controls him, not he his gift....The mere fact of being a man means 'possessing'....The attainment of manhood implies a mastery of one's resources....The charm of the child's productions comes of their being foreign to his will; once his will intervenes, it ruins them. We may expect anything of the child, except awareness and mastery....The art of childhood dies with childhood."

In the pre-school years visual art can be taught primarily for the pleasure it affords the child and as an introduction to the language of vision. But from the point at which serious instruction begins — where the better and the worse ways of using this language are understood as the watershed between what is and what is not true visual art — the pleasure principle alone can't be the primary one by which art education proceeds.

Everychild's art education can teach him to make visual observations with some comprehension; it can teach him the techniques of art; it can teach him to look at works of art appreciatively. But every true artist must teach himself his own art because only he himself can formulate the terms of his quarrel with and his gratitude for existing art; and only he himself can make the language that is common to all become his own distinctive mode of expression.

An artist is able to compose his work because in some essential way he has been able to compose his world — if only to query it pertinently, attack it effectively, or celebrate it joyfully and powerfully. How could the student at the beginning stage of his education possess what it takes of mind and heart, of technical and imaginative power, to command the language in his own right?

The visual artist is a poet of visual ideas. Children cannot be genuine artists in any of the liberal arts until they grow beyond the limitations of childhood. By exaggerating their powers for sentimental reasons, we are more likely to neglect teaching them what they need to know.

To say the least, this point of view is not the prevailing one in the current teaching of art to children. "Natural expression," wrote Herbert Read, "has its own instinctive form, and this would seem to suggest that the aim of education should be to seize on this innate sense of discipline, in order to develop and mature it, rather than to impose on the child a system of discipline which may be alien to its nature and harmful to its mental growth."

Of course a particular system of discipline may be alien to a child's nature. But for good or ill, all systems of education are committed to one or another kind of discipline.

The question is not whether children can, by "natural expression," produce "instinctive form," or whether the "innate sense of discipline" is to be superseded by a kind of discipline not innate (and, presumably, injurious); but, rather, which kind of discipline is the best that education can provide. There must be something that art education can do for the student other than get out of his way.

School's premature elevation of the child to Artist rank has, like Russian roulette, a too easily predictable result. Even the immediate spark of interest is no longer forthcoming when the means of igniting it into a more lasting flame are consistently absent. Nursery school children take to fingerpainting more enthusiastically than eighth-graders to the "natural expression" of doodling.

In *Children Are Artists*, Professor Daniel M. Mendelowitz warns against "mature aesthetic goals" and "high standards of craftsmanship." He declares that "such qualities may be desirable, but only when the child feels they are needed to express what he has to say, when they are not restrictive, and when they do not become ends in themselves."

However, if the child isn't ever taught high standards of craftsmanship, how will he ever know whether or not he needs them to express what he has to say? Moreover, he won't know what he has to say until he has first acquired the means with which to say it.

In art education the goals for a child are no different from that for an adult: to observe, to discern, to interpret. But by anointing the child an "artist" before his time, we lessen the possibility of it really happening.

Learning the techniques of a language is of course restrictive at first; but in time — and education takes time, sometimes a lifetime — the freedom of the student is not curtailed thereby but enhanced. He is free to do more than he could before. What freedom of any worth can the ignorant, undisciplined mind exercise? The all-too-familiar, mindless school student can do nothing, wants to do nothing — except escape. This is despair, not education, as classroom boredom, misbehavior, drop-outs, amply testify. In virtually every aspect of School, the serious approach to learning is the road not taken.

Know-how, skill, craftsmanship, techniques, strengthen intelligence and imagination, not deplete them; even as native faculties increase competence of performance.

The Natural Expression school puts the child's education into his own hands. He may not know what he is doing or why he is doing it, but those who favor this method do not think that he is disadvantaged thereby. The child is father to the man and must not, it is thought by School philosophy, be contaminated by rigorous discipline, radical inquiry, reflective thinking.

Meanwhile, the precious years slip past and the child is obliged to make up his world anyhow. Keeping the child's mind a blank until he can fill in all the important places himself is an especially magnetic notion when it is not known what else to do with it. Then if his mind becomes a discontented blank and life in school grows increasingly incomprehensible, cheerless, and intimidating, who can he blame for his failure but himself?

That this philosophy results in ignorance, incompetence, and the unholy boredom of being free to do, but knowing naught of what to do and wherewith to do comes to us as no surprise by now. Anything is possible, it's Saturday night, but how to use one's freedom is the problem.

Between being so restrictive that the innocent vision of the child is spoiled, and being so permissive that he never learns to use the language of visual art competently, there is — there must be — a happy mean.

That it is possible to teach Everychild the discipline and techniques of a language without at the same time blasting in him the freedom that he will need to use it as an art is not beyond belief. Education can no more "produce" artists than it can happiness or moral virtue. But there is a peculiar irony in the doctrine that not even high standards of craftsmanship should be taught the student except "when the child feels they are needed."

If the school student in his musical studies "should be guided to think of music in the way the finest musicians do," why should he not in the study of visual art be guided to think in the way the finest visual artists do?

The double standard of teaching — one for the School student and the other for the real practitioners of the art — works the same fraud here as elsewhere that it is applied.

In Never Never Land, where it is always Now, the child need never learn anything difficult. Peter Pans flourish. How unlucky for Everychild to be permitted only his natural expression!

What Everychild needs is to grow up, not sideways; what he needs as the core of his education are the skills and arts of language. To lack the appropriate means of expression is to insure a desert where a garden might bloom. But only as an adult does one learn what has been lost in not having learned what he could and should as a child.

What more could one wish for the elementary education of a child but that, standing on the threshold of life, he has acquired the languages he will need to signify his rage and voice his praise, and that he has acquired these well?

Chapter X
LIBERAL EDUCATION FOR ALL

Children will always have different abilities, different kinds of home, different fates in experience. But it is still the duty of government and parents to battle with luck, to try to give the equal chance. And the front of that battle is education...and what I am arguing is that it can't be too good.

Joyce Cary

How to provide Everychild with the best possible elementary education is the most important educational problem in America today.

It is also the most difficult because either it is assumed that this kind of education is already being provided, and therefore there is no such problem; or it is known that the problem exists but it is thought that the deficiencies of early schooling are being corrected somewhere along the line — if not in elementary school, then in high school; if not in high school, then in college; if not in college, then in graduate school; or, finally it is understood that indeed this problem exists, but it is not known how to solve it.

Can the fundamental and essential elements of a real education be given to Everychild?

If the answer to this question is No, nothing in the present School mish-mash would have to be changed. Children in our schools are not getting the kind of education they should be getting; and if, in fact, this cannot be given them, we can go right on doing essentially what we are doing right now. We will continue to try to improve the system by a reading machine, or programmed instruction, or modular scheduling, or dial access systems — or by some other kind of gimmick or gadget, as long as it's trendy. But a gimmick is a gimmick and even with a gadget shall in no wise add up to a genuine elementary education.

If the answer to this question is Yes, and if we think it matters enough to provide our children with a good education, then there is hardly anything in the present system, short of the custodial service, that would not have to be changed.

We have not even begun to give an education of this quality to all children in our nation. We do not know whether or not we can until we try. But it seems reasonable that we can; and it seems more than reasonable — essential — that if we can, we should.

A parent might only discover after six or eight or twelve years of his child's life have been spent in School, that the actual results, measured by appropriate criteria of Education, are — for the time, money, and effort invested — astonishingly and appallingly slight.

A school student's lack of interest in schooling is not necessarily proof that he lacks intelligence, imagination, aptitude, or even desire, for learning. Increasingly, nearly everyone in our society has come to see the connection between a grossly incompetent School system and the consequent incompetence of its students.

The failure of the schools is the failure to educate. Who could blame those students, especially the brighter ones, who are unwilling or unable to give themselves whole-heartedly to employing years of their lives in so evidently losing a proposition?

School officials respond indignantly to the suggestion that there is a cause and effect connection between teacher incompetence and student incompetence. Their journals cite various reasons for the decline of academic achievement in the nation's schools, but conspicuous for its absence is any mention of responsibility that School administrators and School teachers may have for this dismal state of affairs.

The confounding of language, the despairing depth of silences, the sterility of disputes in our society, are social, political, economic, cultural — as well as educational — symptoms. The questions they raise are larger than education alone can resolve. But given the importance of education to youngsters, if the schools and colleges could provide a genuine education, young people might not be as hard put to find clearer and better meanings for their lives.

When communication breaks down, so does community. The liberal arts of good communication are the most important contribution that education can make toward the building of a good community.

Beginning in elementary school, liberal education has two crucial objectives: (1) learning to understand the best works of visual art, music, science, mathematics, literature, at the appropriate levels and according to the student's highest abilities; and (2) learning to participate — by speaking and listening — in discussion about these works.

These are two relatively simple criteria by which any institution professing to be genuinely educational (in the liberal arts sense of the term) may be evaluated.

In the course of achieving these objectives and the skills they require, it is entirely possible that, with rigorous and knowledgeable teaching, something about learning to write the English language at least competently may also be acquired.

Furthermore, it is also entirely possible that increasing the student's grasp of outstanding works in the several languages of learning, and teaching him to discuss these on a rational basis, may also increase his ability to communicate better in both personal and public discourse.

If most young Americans are ineducable in any serious meaning of the term "educate," then there is no problem of quality in education with which we need concern ourselves.

But are young Americans simply born this way? Their apparent indifference to learning and their supposed lack of academic talent and interest may be only the result of the educational desert in which they have been trapped since Grade One.

At what point in a child's life and on what evidence is it to be determined, that he is of the wrong type to acquire a decent education?

Students are not driven into the sea of anti-intelligence by some unaccountable urge. It is not inconceivable that those who are indifferent and incompetent learners acquire their disabilities primarily in School, which is a vast machinery for the cultivation of incompetence and indifference.

Providing a first-rate elementary education for Everychild has never been seriously tried. Only after a reasonable period of trial and in a vastly different kind of learning situation than the present one — and only after it has incontestably failed — can we then begin to think about what else can be done if this educational goal is really impossible.

But as of now, there is no evidence that genuine education for all is impossible. There is every reason to think that it is not only possible but reasonable, practicable, and even necessary.

The American people have never lost sight of or faith in this vision of education for all children. Americans, more than any other people in history, have tended, instinctively and stubbornly, to understand that if this vision is an illusion, so is democracy.

The idea of democracy and the idea of education — liberal education, genuine education — each requires the other for its own fulfillment.

It may be that no school that ever was or ever will be could hold the interest of a Huck Finn. But maybe this is because Aunt Polly or the Widow Douglas is in the superintendent's seat. Given the appreciation that Huck is not stupid, not corrupt, not emotionally disturbed, the way might be found to hold his interest.

The opening chapter of his chronicle, it will be remembered, describes the widow and her sister, Miss Watson, who endeavor to instruct Huck in Deportment. ("Don't gap and stretch like that, Huckleberry — why don't you try to behave?") and Eschatology ("all about the bad place") and the intimate relation between the two. (The "bad place" in the contemporary School ethos is where the student fails to get into the college of his choice, leading to the job of his choice; or where, without a high school diploma, he cannot even get a job, much less one of his choice.) The curriculum is Schoolsville. When Huck retires to his room for the evening, "I felt so lonesome," he says, "I most wished I was dead....Pretty soon I heard a twig snap down in the dark amongst the trees — something was a-stirring. I set still and listened.

Directly I could just barely hear a 'me-yow! me-yow' down there. That was good! Says I, 'me-yow! me-yow' as soft as I could, and then I put out the light and scrambled out of the window on to the shed. Then I slipped down to the ground and crawled in among the trees, and sure enough, there was Tom Sawyer waiting for me."

It was Tom Sawyer; it was life; it was the great escape. Not escape? What else is there to do, faced by the dismal prospect of servitude with the Widow Douglasses and Miss Watsons of this world? How else should he be delivered out of their terrible, well-meaning hands?

It was life and light that Huck was after. He wasn't one to turn from where they were, but neither was he one to linger where they weren't. The Original Young American Hero and School Dropout.

Of course there is always the boy who would not like school under any circumstances, no matter how good it is. He is the independent-minded, the eccentric, the genius, the weak, the dull, or the undisciplined. But for whatever reason, he is Odd Boy Out. The school-room is not for him. The best of schools will often seem somewhat less exciting to a young and lively imagination than floating down the Mississippi, and outer space more inviting than inner. School will be somewhat School in even the best of educational circumstances; and a sweet spring morning, by oneself or with congenial companions, doing nothing or just fooling around, will seem more interesting than anything that could possibly happen in the classroom.

But that's a problem of Life, not of Education. The interests of the two do not always and necessarily coincide. "The low standards of education he achieved," writes J. W. N. Sullivan of Beethoven, "seems to have been as much due to his lack of plasticity as to his lack of opportunities. He was not an educable man."

Society has the obligation to provide all children with the best education that is compatible with their ability, and the obligation not to sell this ability short. But there are those who rightly trust more in their own experience than society's, who take a lonely way, who are not educable as society understands the term. For these exceptional individuals, all that a democratic and compassionate society can decently do is let them develop in their own way.

"As soon as age permitted me to emerge from the control of my tutors, I entirely quitted the study of letters. And resolving to seek no other science than that which could be found in myself, or at least in the great book of the world, I employed the rest of my youth in travel...in collecting various experiences, in proving myself in the various predicaments in which I was placed by fortune....For it seemed to me that I might meet with much more truth in the reasonings that each man makes on the matters that specially concern him, and the issue of which would very soon punish him if he made a wrong judgment, than in the issue of those made by a man of letters in his study touching speculations which lead to no result...."

Huckleberry Finn might have said that if Descartes hadn't beat him to it. And Tocqueville, in the same vein, observes: "In most of the operations of the mind, each

American appeals only to the individual effort of his own understanding.

"America is therefore one of the countries where the precepts of Descartes are least studied and are best applied....The Americans do not read the works of Descartes because their social condition deters them from speculative studies, but they follow his maxims, because this same social condition naturally disposes their minds to adopt them."

The qualities that make for eminence do not always accommodate well to an institution, least of all to the typical School. Moreover, a boy of good intelligence and high spirit is more likely to rebel when there is much there for him to rebel against, even though he may not have coolly and knowledgeably analyzed the situation. His own imagination feels the lack of imagination, his own intelligence the lack of intelligence, confronting him. He may hate the place but still be a learner; still, for example, love to read.

The students who drop out of school are not in general of lesser intelligence than those who remain. However, for whatever reason, they want out.

Is it any mystery why public confidence in the schools has never in our history been lower than it is now? In the sixties it was mainly the college students who thought the School mentality bankrupt (even though they had little or no valid notions as to what to put in its place) but now nearly everyone thinks it.

Some young people do not want more education than the law requires, and would not want it no matter how much the schools improved. Dropouts will be with us always, part of the inevitable untidiness of existence. Since the law in most states does not require a young person to attend school beyond his sixteenth year, what can he do after this age if he does not go to school? If he can find a job, he can go to work. If he cannot find a job (as an untrained worker), he might be able to find one if he were properly trained.

There is no real conflict between liberal education and vocational training, providing both are given their just due, at the right time and in the right place.

Every child needs the best education he can get. He also needs to be trained in a vocation. Those young persons not continuing their academic studies after age sixteen should be assured of vocational schooling at trade schools, community colleges, or on-the-job training, in a marketable skill.

Education, it is said, should prepare the child for life. No doubt it should. What is the alternative — except perhaps for after-life? But what should a child learn in order to be prepared in this way? There is a time for acquiring liberal arts and there is a time for learning a vocation — although putting it this way makes the division between them seem sharper than it need be. But no matter what vocation he comes eventually to follow, (or how many), he will not identify himself solely with it or with them. How else he will come in time to understand himself is not predictable; but it is safely predictable that however else he does, he will be advantaged in having first acquired the fundamentals of a liberal education.

All students are not of course equally intelligent. But the constitutional right of all to equal treatment under the law has the same moral and spiritual root as the right of all children to equal access to a decent elementary education.

Other factors, such as motivation, being equal, the intelligence and imagination that are common to all, albeit in different degree, are educable in all proportionately to the quality of the means used to educate.

It is the rare child who does not at least begin his schooling with a powerful desire to learn. It is the even more rare school that knows how to make good use of this desire. "All men," writes Aristotle, "desire *by nature* to know."(italics added) But, obviously, our public schools in general are more successful in crippling, or at least discouraging, this desire in their students than inspiring it.

Whatever is done to improve Everychild's mind is as worthwhile to him in his life as is the like benefit to his "gifted" classmate. The great and good books that are none too good for the bright ones are none too good for all.

Gifted children must be spared their gifts having to fit a bed of mediocrity. But so must the student of ordinary talent. Books fit only for mental pygmies are no good for anyone else.

It is not the line between "gifted" and "non-gifted" children that the schools must draw, but the line that distinguishes the best in all children to which an education of excellence can be given from the worst in all to which it cannot.

The gifted child in Everychild is the real object of education.

That all children are born gifted — that is, with gifts of intelligence and imagination — may be a fiction, but it is an amiable one. If we assume it from the beginning of Everychild's education, time is less likely to prove it in error. This assumption will surely do more to encourage incentive than the assumption that the gift of learning is bestowed at birth and only upon the favored few.

The incentive is half the battle. Treating a frog as a prince may be just the right way to turn him into one if he has any potential at all in that direction.

In each of the languages of learning the student discovers an entire range of new ideas that can only be known in and through the language itself.

The student proceeds to his education through the portals of language — aptitude or IQ tests notwithstanding. One might as well sum up a child's innate capacity for love or beauty — to each of which, in the depth, dignity, and mystery of his person, his intelligence is bound — as to predict his capacity for new ideas when they are intelligently presented to him in the best forms of language appropriate to his age. Intelligence is not best known by I.Q. or S.A.T. scores.

Education generates its own power. What an infant of "ordinary" intelligence at birth can subsequently learn depends to an overwhelming extent upon what and how he is subsequently taught. (The term "ordinary" is put in quotes in this sentence because, except for those infants afflicted with certain kinds of mental retardation, we cannot know the potential and future intelligence of any new-born child.)

The more ideas that Everychild acquires, through the languages of learning, the more "readings" of human experience he can express; the more readings, the more hope of understanding. How can we predict of Everychild the readings of his life that he may some day make, providing his education gives him the languages with which to make them?

The power of language is the power of intelligence itself. To withhold its serious study from all but the "academically talented" is like withholding jobs from the unemployed because they are poor.

Provide a student with an increased capacity of language — sometimes only a new word — and to that extent you have increased his power of thought. "Bilingual children," wrote the noted neurologist Wilder Penfield, "at the ten-year level in Montreal showed greater intelligence than unilingual children of the same age." Teach the student a foreign tongue, a mathematical notation, a competence in music or visual art, and what is this if not the nurturing of intelligence?

Of course it is possible to be stupid in a half dozen languages. The learned fool is classic. But that's another problem, the answer to which, on good authority, is not the burying of our talents — or those of our children.

Everychild has an initial capital of intelligence that gives him a vested interest in acquiring more. Some children need a little more time to learn than others. On the elementary level, in respect to the limited objectives of the curriculum, that is the essential difference between the "ordinary" and the "gifted" child. Who can foresee which ugly duckling will turn into a swan?

Children of the same age have more in common in respect to their education than they have significant differences. Segregating them in "track" or "grouping" systems by their respective gifts is as much lacking in justification as segregating them by skin color, and not infrequently practiced along the same lines.

Liberal education creates a *community* of learning. The "bright" as well as the "ordinary" benefit from the creation of this community. Moreover, the several languages of learning call upon radically different ways of exercising intelligence and imagination, so that it by no means follows that a child who is superior to his classmates in one of the languages of learning — in mathematics, for example — will be superior to them in all.

Furthermore, in the class discussion of a book that is good enough to provide several depths and various nuances of interpretation, the kinds and quality of contribution made by individual members of the class are not by any means determined entirely by the "intelligence" (as measured by an I.Q. test) of each individual participant; they are also much affected by the individual experience of each and by the effort that each is willing and able to invest in the enterprise.

An essential part of the educational process is the development of the ability to listen and to learn from others. That students in the same class who are of varying degrees of intelligence can learn from each other in the discussion of a good book is not only a fundamental proposition of intellectual courtesy; it is also a fundamental fact of intellectual life.

In a class of students of approximately the same age but of varying degrees of intelligence (assuming all to be at least "ordinary"), insight into the interpretation of a book is no less dependent upon the respective interests, experience, and degree of attention given by the participants to reading it, as upon their respective degrees of intellectual development.

"Learning is a cooperative enterprise," declares the St. John's College *catalog*, "and it is best carried out when persons at different stages of comprehension work together. The typical learning situation at St. John's involves a small group of learners. First in line come the great teachers, the writers of great books, who are talking in most cases at the high point of their learning. Next come the reading and talking teachers, the Tutors, who are members of the faculty; in their stage of learning they are somewhere between the authors and the best students. There then follow the other students at distances proportional to the degree of their understanding....The aim in all the classes is to exploit the differences in knowledge, character, and skill as they are distributed among students and Tutors."

No reasonable opportunity should be denied the more intelligent and no unreasonable demand made upon the less. But it is not any more reasonable for the schools to segregate students in "multi-track" groups or "streaming"arrangements than it would be on the college level. Students of diverse talents can all profit from reading and discussing the same good book, even though all will not understand it equally well or in the same way.

Each child can find his own intellectual level in the same work, if it is good enough, and yet each learn from it enough to be able profitably to discuss the book together with others in the class.

A classroom ought to be a repertory company, not a vehicle for stars. The student learns best by learning together with others. Beyond a certain point, the individual struggle, the lonely quest of heart and mind, the single destiny that is true for one and one only, become the arena of truth. But an educational institution ought to be a place for all to learn together; a place to develop a community of learning, not a training camp for academic warfare. In School environs education is hardly conceived of apart from grades and tests. The brooding, ubiquitous presence of testing and grading cannot help but depress whatever intrinsic motivation the substance of learning is capable of generating on its own.

Because children learn from each other as well as from their teachers and books,

Everychild needs the widest practicable spectrum of talent and intelligence in the children of his own age who are in his class. In a genuine community of learning each member has the responsibility to teach according to his gifts as well as the right to learn according to his needs.

If a child is to participate in the discussion of a book, he must first have read the book. The primary — but not exclusive — motives for his wanting to read it and to participate in its discussion are: one, it is a good book; and two, it is a good discussion. There must be some recognition, some place given, in the education of Everychild for the learning that is its own pleasure and reward.

Elementary education should provide at any one grade level the same books and studies to be pursued by all concurrently, even though all children of the same age will not derive the same value from them. As to this, who can predict the benefit of reading and discussing a work whose echoes might reverberate in one's mind for a lifetime?

Even the teacher needs the opportunity in the classroom to learn as well as to teach. Everyone in the class has both the potentiality and the responsibility of bringing his own insight to the reading of a book.

The ability of each should mean — and be interpreted to mean — responsibility to others as well as opportunity for oneself. Let each communicate to others what he knows better than they; he will learn from them in other ways.

To the extent that School generates and stimulates Grade Fever, it subverts the idea that learning and competence are good in themselves, and it places itself at cross-purpose with the idea that education takes place best within a genuine community of learning.

If grades are what is prized, it is not knowledge, understanding, and wisdom that will be valued. School's obsession with grades is a proof of comic, not serious, intent: it is an alien and spurious substitute for intrinsic interest. The youthful heart and mind reject the alien and spurious; or, what is worse, do not reject them.

A student is either prepared to go on to more advanced work or he is not. In a liberal education — where the idea of community takes precedent over the idea of competition — the student would receive his diploma at the end of a ten-year program when he has demonstrated clearly-designated competencies in each of the four languages of learning: words, mathematics, music, and visual art.

If a diploma is to mean anything much beyond mere attendance, it must stand for learning that is specific and significant. In present School circumstances, who can know what academic achievement a diploma stands for?

Inappropriate competition dissolves the communal bond. It deprives the student of the psychological support of being part of a learning situation where he is helped by his fellow-students according to their strengths even as he may help them according to his.

Keen competition in sports and games is not only appropriate but essential.

However, even here we recognize that if it subverts team play it becomes counter-productive. The reader can undoubtedly supply his own examples of the competitive principle applied unreasonably, where it is harmful and meaningless: but one would be hard put to think of an extensive use for it in the business of getting a good education.

Education seeks both to enhance the self and to build a community of learning. The best education is possible in a good community and the best community is possible only where all have access to genuine education.

Contrary to School philosophy, grades are not the *sine qua non* of all learning. We learn a great deal in life without being graded for it. The experience itself is the grade. In School never have so many been graded so much and with so little learning to show for it. When the end-product is so thin, superficial, and trivial, it seems bizarre that so much weight should be given to the measure of its attainment. One of the momentous events of educational history will undoubtedly occur when it is discovered that learning is possible otherwise.

A little learning is not only a dangerous but a boring thing. In speaking of the schools of his own childhood, John Dewey asked: "How many students were rendered callous to ideas, and how many lost the impetus to learn because of the way in which learning was experienced by them?...How many came to associate the learning process with ennui and boredom?" That School is dreadfully dull is an educational scandal about which we hear all to little, perhaps because those who are its customary victims are considered the least qualified to report it in a way to gain credence.

This is a great big wide beautiful world — yes, indeed — but School is not noted for the power to astonish by its representation of it. Since its version is too dull for a young person to believe in, School creates the oldest credibility gap known. Consequently, the youngster feels the urge to drop out and discover for himself whether the world is as dismal as his classroom experience makes it seem.

Induced stupidity is as endemic to the schools today as in John Dewey's childhood. By under-estimating the student's intelligence, the schools bore him; by boring him, they dull his faculties; with dulled faculties the child confirms School's low estimate of his intelligence. And so forth and so dreary Schoolday on. "A large percentage of the Nation's 5.5 million retarded have low IQs simply because they never have had any mental stimulation during the years when their brains were developing," said Dr. Stafford Warren, an authority on mental retardation. He went on to say that "even youngsters with potentially high IQs will join the ranks of the retarded in such a climate of cultural deprivation."

Is it any wonder that parents should feel rage at how School fails their children?

Intelligence, retarded or not, tends to rise or fall according to the level of intelligence extended to it. The proposition that an authentic education is only for the academically talented obscures the even more important — and more demonstrable

— proposition that what the child is capable of learning depends to a considerable extent upon what he has already learned and what he is thought capable of learning if properly taught.

Which comes first, the learning or the intelligence to learn? Clearly, a chicken-and-egg proposition. But this much at least ought to be self-evident. Take the child at his highest bent — his greatest, not his least, potential — and of course he is more likely to come in a learner.

We don't know a great deal about retardation, but we do know that moronic schooling cannot be ruled out altogether as a possible cause.

The principle runs throughout the learning process: If competent teaching and a reasonable ratio between the learner and the learning material be assumed, then mastery develops in proportion to the power of what is to be mastered. Or, to put it in another and more specific way: The more that is required of a child who is capable of higher achievement, the better the educational results.

Schools that grossly under-estimate the ability of their students stunt the very faculties that they are responsible for developing. Typically, then, School points to the resultant non-student as an example of how difficult it is to teach him — and his kind — successfully.

School provides the purest and most notorious example known of a vicious circle. It mis-educates or non-educates and then asks, How is it possible to educate the likes of *them*?

After School has wasted years of his life, a student may well feel that he is uneducable.

How many students do we find, even at the college and university levels, who have no "mathematical aptitude" or no "musical aptitude" or no "aptitude" for poetry or visual art, and therefore believe themselves unable to learn these disciplines?

But teach Everychild the languages of learning from the First Grade — and teach him well — and he may never discover that they are beyond him. How well they can be learned by a particular student depends upon a variety of factors, not least of which is the competence of his teachers to teach them.

Exactly when in the history of education those feelings of ennui and boredom that John Dewey mentions, and that so many children associate with learning, first began — probably some time in the Old Stone Age — that they do not necessarily accompany education was assumed by Dewey and is assumed by all serious educators.

If a teacher doesn't know how to teach well — and the reader is invited to try recalling exactly how many teachers stimulated his intelligence and imagination in the course of his own School career — he jumps readily to the conclusion that his students are either naturally stupid or naturally delinquent.

Although stupidity is known to exist among school children — as indeed among teachers also — the schools appear unduly tempted to let this insight dominate their philosophy. Until School itself becomes less stupid, it will not be able to tell with fine discrimination what is stupidity in the student and what is simply an understandable response to the School environment.

The relation between disorderly behavior and boredom in the schools is obvious. Disorder results from boredom, and boredom results from not having anything to do that matters. (Needless to say, the situation is not always this simple; other social and personal factors are revelant too. But the schools must be held responsible for those educational factors that they do control.) Happily, the solution to both problems — misbehavior and miseducation — would appear the same for both. What stimulates intelligence and imagination is not boring and is educational.

In comparison to the magniloquence of statements typical of School objectives, that of being rarely bored may not seem to be saying a great deal. Be that as it may, whatever other problems of existence present themselves to a student, it is not likely that as a young citizen of golden realms boredom will be one of them.

The more inappropriately we set our educational goals, the more difficult it becomes to educate anyone properly. Only by attempting to provide the best possible education for all children will we succeed in providing it for any. Most of the present School jumble is either wasteful, fraudulent, inadequate, or ineffective. So little is learned in comparison to what ought and might be learned in those crucial years.

The death of the mind is death's most significant sign. We label a large majority of our school students "non-academic" or unintelligent when School has not known how to use their minds in vital ways.

Relegate these students to the dunce row at the back of the room and you tell them that in the academic environment they are not wanted — a euphemism for "dead." We ought not then be surprised if their response to this doesn't come up to drawing-room standards. "Even a dog," wrote Justice Oliver Wendell Holmes, "distinguishes between being stumbled over and being kicked."

In a discussion of civil rights, a representative of HARYOU (Harlem Youth Opportunities Unlimited) declared: "I want my child *educated*. If integration means putting whites and blacks together but still teaching the blacks as if they can't learn what the whites can, I don't need that kind of integration. Sure, social experience between white and black is a wonderful thing to learn, but by itself integration doesn't fill my child's basic needs. The way it is now, black kids, whether they're in integrated schools or not, are being drained of their motivating forces. They become the 'niggers' the whites tell them they are."[Italics his]

In affirming the idea of the liberal arts for all, allowance must be made for those children who are distracted from learning by severe emotional or other serious personal problems. The education of a child is disadvantaged by all circumstances of life that are irrational, wounding, frustrating, wasteful, sterile, boring, or unjust. It is at least open to question, however, whether even these children would not benefit more from an education that provides them with the fundamentals of learning — as much of it as they can get — than they do from a bastard version of education that provides them with the fundamentals of little or nothing; and which must, in fact, by its very emptiness add to their problems.

The schools do no favor to a child from a broken, unhappy, or disadvantaged home if, to the injury he has already received from life, they add the insult of treating him as a lamebrain.

The best education, the same liberal arts for all, is one way that society can make up in part for the private, irrational, fortuitous, and disabling circumstances of life.

Even on the dubious assumption that it is only the best who deserve the best, there is no way to tell in the tender years of childhood who are to be the future leaders and benefactors of humanity; we cannot know whom we deprive of the best — in fact, whom we keep from possible greatness — if we do not give at least the rudiments of the best to all.

"Every human being," said Pope John XXIII, "has the right to a basic education...." If we don't know the difference between Schooling and Education, how can we provide children this right?

A liberal education for all is the test of the seriousness with which we battle for educational excellence. Slough off the "non-academic type" and the lower ranks of those who remain are the next to go. A legitimate education only for the privileged few, the academic elite, is a losing proposition all along the line.

Would such an education as this book describes, be the best kind of education for children of the slums?

No, not if we thought to keep them in the slums all their lives.

Yes, if we had it in mind to help them get out of the slums and to get the slums out of them.

The worst of the many injustices inflicted upon children of poverty is the effect of the assumption, that because they live in poor housing, they are only capable of a poor education.

Culturally deprived home — culturally deprived schooling — culturally deprived second-generation home — describes the vicious circle in which these American children are caught.

The schools cannot do anything about eliminating social conditions that clearly have an adverse effect on the learning abilities of those children who have to live under them. But then they are not asked to do anything about adverse economic and social conditions. They are asked...and asked...and asked...to do something about the educational conditions that prevail within their own bailiwick.

The School as Center of Intellectual and Imaginative Poverty is something about which schools have the responsibility to do a great deal.

The greater the failure of the schools in solving educational problems, the more avidly they have turned to non-educational answers. Educational problems during the 1940s and 1950s were commonly transmogrified into psychiatric ones. Educational theorists who took the most pessimistic view of what could be done for a child's mind were most optimistic about what could be done for his psyche. We were not likely to wake up some morning and discover that everything that we ever knew about how to bring up a child was all wrong — nor did we. But depth psychology and its numerous and various offshoots persuaded many that we did. Many, many moons ago, by the shores of Gitche Gumee, it was thought that understanding was a gift of grace or a triumph of mind or heart, not a game in which any number could play if only equipped with the latest psychiatric jargon.

It is no longer generally held that education must look to the prophets of mental health for leadership. "Psychoanalysis," wrote Bruno Bettelheim, "has little to offer when it comes to reforming education."

In the 1960s, 1970s, and 1980s sociology was in the saddle. The failure of the schools was "explained" as a failure of the social environment, particularly the family. Even pre-school learning, we were told, was so important that if a child's intellectual life at home had been neglected during pre-school years, he would probably be ineducable by age six. "Substantial studies of school achievement," declared Robert J. Havighurst, then a professor of education at the University of Chicago, "in relation to family socio-economic status show that the family environment is more important than the school in determining a child's educational achievement."

Do we really have to solve the socio-economic problems of the country before we can address ourselves seriously to solving the educational ones? Some families are indeed loaded with socio-economic problems and have no immediately realistic hope of unloading them, but who want in the meantime a decent education for their children.

In general, educational effects are primarily determined by educational causes. It is not an unknown experience that children from poor families are capable of acquiring a good education when the opportunity is given them.

The school student may be described in sociological terms or as a psychological type, but it is always and only a single self who is to be educated. As to his education, Everychild does not fit into any pigeon-holes. Education occurs to each life individually. But, obviously, his educational opportunities are crucial to his experience.

Suppose a child's family environment to be an intellectual and cultural wasteland — no books, no music, no art, no science, no significant intellectual or artistic experience of any kind. How would this fact alone prevent him from learning art, music, mathematics, science, languages — if the schools were competent to teach these to him?

Who has not heard of persons who grew up in families that were indifferent or even antagonistic to their intellectual development and who nevertheless managed by means of some resources, in themselves or in the community, to escape their family's dead hand?

It is not only inner city children who live in an intellectual desert. The main extrcurricular cultural diet for many middle and upper class suburban children consists of the trashiest kind of television programs and other varieties of Fun. A lively intellectual and imaginative atmosphere in the schools could help Everychild's escape from cheap entertainment obsessions.

But "a lively intellectual and imaginative atmosphere" does not describe the typical American school today. The child of ordinary intelligence who has not learned to read well is more likely to be a victim of School than of either his family's socio-economic status or of being born a "non-academic type."

To admit a correlation between educational achievement and family status may be admitting to no more than that poor children are usually taught in poor schools; the better schools are usually to be found in the richer school districts —which would come as a revelation to no one.

Learning how to read well will not fill a child's stomach, it will not compensate him for the lack of a parent's love, it will not solve race problems. It is only the most important reason for a school's existence.

The primary issues of education have to do with teaching and learning, learning and teaching. If we conceive of the primary issues as busing versus non-busing, centralization versus decentralization, professional versus lay control, local authority versus State or Federal authority — as important as these and other related questions may be — it isn't likely that with the resolution of these and similar questions alone, that we shall be able to create an educational system that really educates. Understanding the nature of education and the principles by which it proceeds are the crucial questions.

Children who are under-nourished can't learn properly. To insure that they are properly nourished is an economic and political problem. But the implication must be firmly rejected that the education of children of the poor would be assured by the present School system once their families' economic needs were met.

The vast majority of children in our society are not underfed and do not live in slums. Nevertheless, it has become increasingly evident that the schools are not really educating anyone. This problem is not only unsolved in our society; it doesn't even begin to be seriously addressed.

The crucial educational issue is the competence of the schools to educate. The family is no academic institution and the schools are no substitute for the family. Each has its own kind of teaching to do, and the failure of the one cannot be justly laid at the door of the other.

It is no more reasonable to think that as a general rule the family environment is more important than School in determining good educational results than that School is more important than the family in determining good family results. The family cannot justly blame the School for the failure of the family to provide an orderly, just, peaceful, loving environment, any more than School can justly blame the family for the failure to provide a sound elementary education.

A family in which there is respect for intellectual and artistic achievement can obviously be a potent educational influence upon its children. On the other hand, even where the intellectual life of a family is, to say the least, meager, who could deny that the schools might be a potent educational influence upon a child of this family, assuming that he was educable and that they knew how to educate.

You never know who might make it if given the chance.

That Everychild may realistically entertain the hope of standing to the fullness of his height depends not a little upon the height to which he is called. The less he is assumed capable of growing, the less that will be done to encourage his growth.

The lower that School supposes it must stoop to educate Everychild, the harder it becomes to reach him.

A good educational system, like a good book, would be more willing to risk over-rating than under-rating intelligence. No one gets it all. "The soul selects its own society." So too does the work of art. But a liberal education for Everychild would at least give his highest potential the chance to select the best and be selected by it.

Everychild's intelligence cannot be known until it has been given the appropriate opportunity to develop and to make itself known. Can anyone believe that School now provides him this opportunity?

Children do not all develop their respective talents equally. But then neither do adults. Simply by virtue of being human, the need for education — the need of all children to extend and to understand better the various meanings of life — is equal in all.

Education is a way not only of understanding life better, and therefore making it more endurable and possibly even more joyous in many ways; it is also a way of enriching life. A liberal education will not provide Everychild with all the meaning that he seeks, but it is a way of helping to prepare him with some of the meaning he needs for his journey.

School makes the victim the cause of the crime. Insult is not only added to injury but becomes ideologically and psychologically indispensable to it. It is always easier to victimize someone if we can first convince ourselves that he deserves no better.

A child is educable for exactly the same reason as an adult — he has a mind.

Intellectual maturity, ripeness of spirit, and experience of life, are pre-requisite to the elementary understanding of certain subjects and to the deeper understanding of all subjects. But education, like a good drama has a beginning, a middle, and an end. Childhood is the time, the exactly right time, for real education to begin.

As soon as Everychild is ready to begin the study of written signs, he is ready to begin his elementary liberal education. It is in the nature of a child's mind to be able to understand the forms of language. The direct experience of good language is not grim to the child, as School assumes. The best and most powerful examples of language that Everychild can be taught is the shortest path to the fulfillment of educational aims.

The parents who send their child to private school do so by exercising a freedom of choice that for obvious economic reasons is not open to all. Maybe it should be. The education of a nation's children is too important to the common good for freedom of choice in selecting a school for Everychild to be denied upon the basis of his parents' lack of means. This isn't the place to discuss the pros and cons of the voucher plan in detail, but it may well be an idea whose time has come.

The education of a child may be said to begin when he is first nursed at his mother's breast. This bond between mother and child will enhance the subsequent development of his learning abilities — which suggests that we don't learn simply with our "minds" but with our entire being.

In the touching, holding, kissing, embracing of his mother (and his father), the child first learns — on his pulse — the goodness and meaning of his life. He first learns through his senses that life is meaningful because it is good. He learns this lesson — fundamental, if any is — physically, emotionally. He begins to read the signs of life in the taste of his mother's milk, in the scent of her flesh, in the touch of her hand, in the sound of her voice, in the sight of her face.

There is no cogent definition of the aims of liberal education that does not apply in some significant sense to the first pre-notational stage of learning. If the child is fortunate in having parents who understand and provide for both the emotional and the rational needs of his nature — loving and learning — in this first stage of life, he may learn more of what it means to be human than he ever will again in a comparable period of time. Nursing an infant — or at any rate, giving him tender loving care in other ways — is a first course in the Humanities.

But if the meaning of liberal education in a more limited sense refers specifically to the study and teaching that the languages of learning make possible; then, clearly, what is meant by the term cannot occur until the child learns to use language in these forms.

When he does, he will be using his mind no differently in kind than when he becomes an adult. If he has made a good beginning, if he has had a good elementary education, he will, as an adult, be able to use language more subtly and powerfully than he ever could as a child. But this is a difference of degree, not of kind.

A child has a mind whose development deserves, as fully as an adult's, profound respect. If we do not respect the potential power of his mind, we will not provide him with the kind of education that he needs in order to develop it as he can and should; and we should not then be surprised if the child becomes an adult with little or no respect for the life of the mind, either his own or anyone else's.

If children are to be educated and not merely Schooled, the American public will have to take a more direct hand in holding School management responsible. This can't be done by remote, sporadic, or inconsistent control.

But neither can it be done without a clear understanding of the results that are appropriate and realistic to expect.

It will no longer do to leave the education of our children solely in the hands of the Professionals. There is always some flim-flammery behind this term, but more in education than anywhere else.

If good management in the making of factory products insists upon quality control, how much more urgent is the control of quality in the education of our children.

The ultimate responsibility for the quality of education in our schools belongs to the ultimate arbiters in our democratic republic: We the People.

The stakes are incalculable: the mind and heart of Everychild.

APPENDIX A

The following is a brief statement that is intended to exemplify how a school based upon a philosophy of elementary liberal education, such as this book defines, might express its specific aims and principles.

THE LIBERAL ARTS SCHOOL
Introduction

E ducation of the young should develop powers of intelligence and imagination that last a lifetime. The liberal arts, which are the substance of a liberal education, are the traditional and most effective way of developing these powers.

The aims of a liberal education are to seek to understand what is most worth understanding and to be able to use effectively the forms of language that are the principal vehicles of understanding.

The liberal arts are the keys to the world of learning. They are the means by which language is used at its best.

The study of language in its several major forms — of words, of mathematics, of music, of visual art — and as exemplified by individual works of art in which these forms are powerfully and characteristically expressed is the main principle by which elementary liberal education here proceeds.

The liberal arts are democratic in nature. Every child is capable of learning to understand and to use them.

Although every child can learn these arts, to at least a modest degree of competence, they can be taught well only by teachers who are themselves liberal artists in the subjects they teach.

Teaching and learning liberal arts constitute the purpose of this school.

The Language of Words

This language is the most important of the means by which human beings communicate with each other. The way to teach the student to use this form of language effectively — in reading, in writing, in speaking, and in listening — is to teach with its best examples.

The best books that the student can be taught to read at each stage of his development are the main highway of this curriculum, and discussion is the predominant method used in teaching them.

The First Grade student here begins to read and to discuss good children's books as soon as he acquires the rudiments of reading — by the phonetic approach.

Beginning in the First Grade, there is daily instruction in a modern foreign language (French). This starts with conversation and progresses as rapidly as possible to the reading of children's literature in this language.

A classical language (Latin) is also studied, beginning in the eighth grade and continuing for three years.

Science education in The Liberal Arts School is studied in the field (or lake or sky); in the laboratory, where simple classic experiments are performed; and in outstanding essays on science.

The Language of Mathematics

In the study of mathematics, arithmetic paves the way. In this preparatory part of mathematical study, the young student gains the preliminary experience with the language out of which concepts, structure, and analysis can develop.

The understanding of structure is come upon only after the mathematical edifice has been lived in for a while.

Timing is of the essence in elementary education. Children should be introduced to the language of mathematics similarly to the way they are taught a modern foreign language; that is, learning its patterns of thought and manner of expression by getting the hang of how it works in practice.

Computational skills are the gateway to the study of mathematics as a liberal art. The primary aims of the entire mathematics program in elementary liberal education — from arithmetic to geometry — should be to enable the student to do elementary mathematics competently and to learn to enjoy the rigorous beauty of its language.

The last three years of the mathematics course are engaged in the study of significant works of mathematical thought, beginning — and continuing for the greater part of three years — with Euclid.

The Language of Music

The study of music is important enough to warrant playing a major role in the elementary liberal arts program.

The most direct and the most effective way to engage the student's interest in music is by teaching him to be a performer. Daily instruction in music performance (including music theory, music history, and the practical knowledge of several different types of musical instruments) is given all students.

The student begins his musical studies in active response to music. He is taught to think of music as a good musician does. Our goal is to provide the fundamentals of a sound music education to all students at this school.

As the student will be a reader all his life if he is taught reading well, from the beginning of his school career; so, too, we believe that he will learn to love and to play music all his life if he is taught music well as a child.

The Language of Visual Art

The principal aim of teaching visual art as an integral part of liberal education is to develop visual intelligence and imagination: to teach the student to look, which is to observe; to see, which is to understand; and to make, which is to interpret and transform.

Part of art education consists in learning how to "read" works of visual art and part in learning how to use the language of vision as a craftsman; not, however, as separate or equal parts, but as one integrated course.

Every student at this school learns rudiments of the language of vision in many different ways — crafts, drawing, painting, photography, calligraphy, sculpture, architecture. By extending the student's competence, the teacher of visual art is able to help him acquire the knowledge of the language that will enable him to express himself more effectively; hence, more freely.

No one can teach the student the visual forms by which he will interpret to himself and to others what he sees and imagines; no one can make of him an Artist. But art education can teach him the craftsmanship that may make it possible for him to discover the forms he wants to make as he acquires the craft and maturity to make them.

Complementary Competencies

Although the curriculum of The Liberal Arts School is built upon the foundation of the four languages of learning, there are other skills taught to every student here that complement the liberal arts program. For example:

Athletics. Every student is given the opportunity, encouragement, and instruction needed to play at least two sports to the best of his or her ability: an individual sport and a team sport. The ancient Greeks understood perhaps better than any people in history that, like the mind, the body functions more freely and more effectively when it is well trained, developed, and cared for.

Manual Skills. The faculties of imagination and intelligence do not exist in a disembodied spirit; we are corporeal creatures (and this too is a reason for thanksgiving).

The Liberal Arts School requires every pupil to learn a manual skill. Cooking, Carpentry, and Gardening are the choices offered.

The Cooking class provides instruction in culinary arts that goes considerably beyond the School "home ec" course.

The Carpentry class emphasizes the application of arithmetic to this practical skill; knowledge of the correct use of various woods and tools; and the artistic values inherent in good construction and design.

The Gardening class, like the other two manual skills, combines science, art, and recreation. Each child that elects this class is responsible for a bit of turf in which to practice some of the answers to the question, How does your garden grow?

Conclusion

This is a ten-year curriculum for the education of children from ages six to sixteen.

Although all students at this school pursue the same program of study — and all students of the same age pursue this program at the same time — those who evidence unusual ability or interest in a particular subject are strongly encouraged, and are provided additional means, to pursue this interest further. Students who evidence weakness in a particular part of the curriculum are given special assistance according to their need.

The Liberal Arts School aims to create a genuine community of learning for all engaged in learning and teaching here. As members of this community, we are not in competition with each other; but, ideally, in communication, striving to overcome the resistance to learning — whether in sloth, prejudice, or closed mind — that exists in all of us, for whatever reason.

The aim of this community is to give all its members the maximum opportunity and encouragement to acquire those forms of language, the skills and arts of communication, that intelligence and imagination need in order to be used effectively and well.

APPENDIX B
BOOKS FOR *THE EDUCATION OF EVERYCHILD*

O f the making of book lists, there is no end.
The reader who would like a simple index of the difference between the quality of reading that children now do in School and the quality that they might be doing should compare the titles on the Junior Great Books list with the Schoolbooks now used to teach reading in American schools.

This list represents a criterion that, to say the least, is not generally found in the schools. The books on this list, or books of comparable caliber, are intended for both reading and discussion.

Good books of this kind should be used not only for "enrichment" or only for "gifted" children, but in a regular reading program for all children.

The titles on this list have been tested by The Great Books Foundation in many discussion groups all over the country.

Some of these books are of course read now by some school students; it would be difficult to avoid them altogether. But, generally speaking (and in fifty states the practice has some diversity), it is the School textbook that is the main academic staple in every school subject. Junk food for the mind: committee-written; cheaply illustrated; lacking literary power or validity; lacking the stamp of individual genius (but not lacking a rigidly restricted, Schoolese vocabulary)— looking like nothing so much as School.

This list is not intended as definitive, comprehensive, or the last word in good or great children's books. It should be supplemented in the curriculum by writing of similar quality from other lists available at any good public library.

THE JUNIOR GREAT BOOKS READING AND DISCUSSION SERIES

The Junior Great Books reading series are collections of outstanding traditional and modern literature. No text is modified to meet a controlled vocabulary.

Series Two through Nine include children's classics, folk and fairy tales, and modern short stores from cultures around the world. Series Ten through Twelve present short selections from great works of philosophy, political science, psychology, and economics, as well as modern fiction. Junior Great Books readings sustain extended discussion because they are rich in ideas. As participants pool their thoughts in discussion, complex works gradually become accessible.

The "Read-Aloud" books for reading to children would be eminently suited for the first year of Everychild's reading curriculum, during which time he is also learning the phonetic method of reading, so that by his second year he is ready to read and discuss the books on Series 2 of the list.

The titles on Series 2-9 would be the primary books for the reading course from the second to the tenth year. Series 10, 11, and 12 could be used to supplement readings in the latter part of this ten-year Program.*

THE READ-ALOUD PROGRAM

Dragon Series
Volume 1
The Frog Prince, Brothers Grimm, as told by Wanda Gag
Guinea Fowl and Rabbit Get Justice, African folktale as told by Harold Courlander
    and George Herzog
"Nature Speaks", Poetry by Carl Sandburg, James Reeves, and Federico
    Garciá Lorca

Volume 2
Feraj and the Magic Lute, Arabian folktale as told by Jean Russell Larson
The Tale of Johnny Town-Mouse, Beatrix Potter
"Companions", Poetry by Robert Louis Stevenson, Gwendolyn Brooks, and
    A.A. Milne

Volume 3
Buya Marries the Tortoise, African folktale as told by W.F.P. Burton
*The Huckabuck Family and How They Raised Pop Corn in Nebraska and Quit and
    Came Back*, Carl Sandburg
"Magical Places", Poetry by Byrd Baylor, William Shakespeare, and Martin Brennan

Sailing Ship Series
Volume 1
The Shoemaker and the Elves, Brothers Grimm, as told by Wanda Gág
The Frog Went A-Traveling, Russian folktale as told by Vsevolod Garshin
"Night into Dawn", Poetry by Robert Hillyer and John Ciardi; and a Mescalero
    Apache song

* For further information about the Great Books Foundation's exercises designed to reinforce reading comprehension, writing, and discussion skills, and the classes in discussion leading offered frequently in locations across the country, write: Great Books Foundation, 35 E. Wacker Dr., Suite 2300, Chicago IL 60601-2298; or call 1-800-222-5870; (312) 332-5870 (in Illinois). FAX 312-407-0334.

Volume 2
The Tale of Two Bad Mice, Beatrix Potter
Bouki Cuts Wood, Haitian folktale as told by Harold Courlander
"Fantasy", Poetry by Edward Lear and Lewis Carroll

Volume 3
Lion at School, Philippa Pearce
Coyote Rides the Sun, Native American folktale as told by Jane Louise Curry
"Seasons", Poetry by Robert Louis Stevenson, Langston Hughes, and Nikki Giovanni

Sun Series
Volume 1
The Black Hen's Egg, French folktale as told by Natalie Savage Carlson
The Mouse and the Wizard, Hindu fable as told by Lucia Turnbull
"Imagination", Poetry by Leslie Norris, Mark Van Doren, and Robert Louis
     Stevenson

Volume 2
Rumpelstiltskin, Brothers Grimm, translated by Ralph Manheim
"Eeyore Has a Birthday and Gets Two Presents", A.A. Milne
"When I Grow Up", Poetry by Rabindranath Tagore and X.J. Kennedy, and
     a Chippewa song

Volume 3
The King of the Frogs, African folktale as told by Humphrey Harman
Snow-White and the Seven Drawfs, Brothers Grimm, translated by Randall Jarrell
"Mysterious Animals", Poetry by T.S. Eliot, Jenifer Kelly, and Robert Graves

Pegasus Series
Volume 1
Chestnut Pudding, Iroquois folktale as told by John Bierhorst
The Pied Piper, English folktale as told by Joseph Jacobs
"Fanciful Animals", Poetry by Edward Lear and A.A. Milne

Volume 2
The Mermaid Who Lost Her Comb, Scottish folktale as told by Winifred Finlay
Hansel and Gretel, Brothers Grimm, translated by Randall Jarrell
"Special Places", Poetry by Gwendolyn Books and Robert Frost, and a Navajo poem

Volume 3
Mother of the Waters, Haitian folktale as told by Diane Wolkstein

Zlateh the Goat, Isaac Bashevis Singer
"Secret Messages", Poetry by Robert Louis Stevenson, Barbara Juster Esbensen, and
    Emily Dickinson

SERIES 2
Two Fables, LaFontaine, Aesop
The Happy Lion, Louise Fatio
Cinderella, Charles Perrault
The Monkey and the Crocodile, Ellen C. Babbitt
The Mouse Bride, Lucia Turnbull**
Stone Soup, Marcia Brown**
The Terrible Leak, Yoshiko Uchida**
How the Camel Got His Hump, Rudyard Kipling
Jack and the Beanstalk, Joseph Jacobs**
The Man with the Wen, Idries Shah**
Tom-Tit-Tot, Flora Annie Steel**
The Velveteen Rabbit, Margery Williams

SERIES 3
The Master Cat (or: Puss-in-Boots), Charles Perrault
The Fisherman and His Wife, Jacob and Wilhelm Grimm**
The Ugly Duckling, Hans Christian Andersen
Caporushes, Flora Annie Steel**
The Monster Who Grew Small, Joan Grant
The Brave Little Tailor, Jacob and Wilhelm Grimm**
Ooka and the Honest Thief, I.G. Edmonds
The Green Man, Gail E. Haley
The Fire on the Mountain, Harold Courlander and Wolf Leslau**
Beauty and the Beast, Madame de Villeneuve
Ellen's Lion, Crockett Johnson
The Mousewife, Rumer Godden

The Black Heart of Indri, Dorothy Hoge
It's All the Fault of Adam, Barbara Walker
Jean Labadie's Big Black Dog, Natalie Savage Carlson
The Little Humpbacked Horse, Post Wheeler
The Jackal and the Partridge, Flora Annie Steel
The Snowman, Hans Christian Andersen
The Tale of the Three Storytellers, James Krüss
Women's Wit, Howard Pyle

                    **Based on traditional material

The Stone Crusher of Banjang, Harold Courlander**
How the Tortoise Became, Ted Hughes
The Invisible Child, Tove Jansson
*The Wind in the Willows**, Kenneth Grahame

SERIES 4
The Red Balloon, Albert Lamorisse
The Emperor's New Clothes, Hans Christian Andersen
The Devoted Friend, Oscar Wilde
Allah Will Provide, Robert Gilstrap and Irene Estabrook**
Vasilissa the Beautiful, Post Wheeler**
Prince Rabbit, A.A. Milne
*The Story of Dr. Dolittle**, Hugh Lofting
The Imp in the Basket, Natalie Babbitt
Mr. Toad, Kenneth Grahame
The Goldfish, Eleanor Farjeon
The Elephant's Child, Rudyard Kipling
Ali Baba and the Forty Thieves, Charlotte Dixon**

How the Donkey and the Elephant Became, Ted Hughes
*The Wicked Tricks of Tyl Uilenspiegel**, Jay Williams
Mr. Singer's Nicknames, James Krüss
The Story of Wang Li, Elizabeth Coatsworth
Thunder, Elephant, and Dorobo, Humphrey Harman**
A Likely Place, Paula Fox
The Enchanted Sticks, Steven J. Meyers
Wisdom's Wages and Folly's Play, Howard Pyle
The Battle of the Frogs and the Mice, George Martin
The Hemulen Who Loved Silence, Tove Jansson
What the Neighbors Did, Philippa Pearce
*Alice's Adventures in Wonderland**, Lewis Carroll

SERIES 5
Charles, Shirley Jackson
The Nightingale, Hans Christian Andersen
Thank you, M'am, Langston Hughes
Fables, Leo Tolstoy
The Happy Prince, Oscar Wilde
Fresh, Philippa Pearce
Echo and Narcissus, Kathleen Lines**

* Selection   **Based on traditional material

All Summer in a Day, Ray Bradbury
Kaddo's Wall, Harold Courlander and George Herzog**
The Fifty-First Dragon, Heywood Broun
Spit Nolan, Bill Naughton
Maurice's Room, Paula Fox

The Ghost Cat, Donna Hill
The Prince and the Goose Girl, Elinor Mordaunt
Podhu and Aruwa, Humphrey Harman**
Lucky Boy, Philippa Pearce
Dita's Story, Mary Q. Steele
Alberic the Wise, Norton Juster
The Secret of the Hattifatteners, Tove Jansson
The White Falcon, Charlton Ogburn
The Mysteries of the Cabala, Isaac Bashevis Singer
The Magic Jacket, Walter de le Mare
Lenny's Red-Letter Day, Bernard Ashley
The Bat-Poet, Randall Jarrell

SERIES 6
Through the Tunnel, Doris Lessing
The Parsley Garden, William Saroyan
The Gun Without a Bang, Robert Sheckley
The Alligators, John Updike
I Don't See George Anymore, Philip Oakes
*The Jungle Book**, Rudyard Kipling
The Zodiacs, Jay Neugeboren
Day of the Butterfly, Alice Munro
The Veldt, Ray Bradbury
A Game of Catch, Richard Wilbur
To Build a Fire, Jack London
As the Night the Day, Abioseh Nicol

SERIES 7
Harrison Bergeron, Kurt Vonnegut, Jr.
The Idealist, Frank O'Connor
The Stone Boy, Gina Berriault
Sir Tristram and the Fair Iseult, Roger Lancelyn Green**
The White Circle, John Bell Clayton

**Based on traditional material

Bad Characters, Jean Stafford
The Cat and the Coffee Drinkers, Max Steele
The Camel, The Lion, The Leopard, The Crow and the Jackal, Ramsay Wood**
Gaston, William Saroyan
The Rocking-Horse Winner, D.H. Lawrence
Sponono, Alan Paton
*The Adventures of Huckleberry Finn**, Mark Twain

SERIES 8
The Ledge, Lawrence Sargent Hall
Sucker, Carson McCullers
The Summer of the Beautiful White Horse, William Saroyan
Rufus, James Agee
Boys and Girls, Alice Munro
A Stick of Green Candy, Jane Bowles
Mateo Falcone, Prosper Mérimée
The Griffin and the Minor Canon, Frank R. Stockton
The Destructors, Graham Greene
Baby Deer, Sunil Gangopadhyaya
Debbie Go Home, Alan Paton
Dr. Jekyll and Mr. Hyde, Robert Louis Stevenson

SERIES 9
The Lottery, Shirley Jackson
A Mystery of Heroism, Stephen Crane
A Bird in the House, Margaret Laurence
Miriam, Truman Capote
The Guest, Albert Camus
The Time Machine, H.G. Wells
End of the Game, Julio Cortázar
Mumu, Ivan Turgenev
The Outlaws, Selma Lagerlöf
The End of the Party, Graham Greene
The Evildoer, Anton Chekhov
The Loneliness of the Long-Distance Runner, Alan Sillitoe

SERIES 10
*Why War?**, Sigmund Freud
*The Melian Dialogue**, Thucydides

* Selection   **Based on traditional material

*The Social Me**, William James
Rothschild's Fiddle, Anton Chekhov
*Concerning the Division of Labor**, Adam Smith
Chelkash, Maxim Gorky
*How an Aristocracy May Be Created by Industry**, Alexis de Tocqueville
*Observation and Experiment**, Claude Bernard
Everything That Rises Must Converge, Flannery O'Connor
*An Essay in Aesthetics**, Roger Fry
An Outpost of Progress, Joseph Conrad
*On Studying**, José Ortega y Gasset

SERIES 11
*Politics**, Aristotle
*Of Commonwealth**, Thomas Hobbes
Barn Burning, William Faulkner
*Of Civil Government**, John Locke
In Exile, Anton Chekhov
The Declaration of Independence
*Equality**, Isaiah Berlin
Sorrow-Acre, Isak Dinesen
*Why Americans Are Often So Restless**, Alexis de Tocqueville
After the Ball, Leo Tolstoy
*Habit**, William James
The Overcoat, Nikolai Gogol

SERIES 12
*On Happiness**, Aristotle
*Habits and Will**, John Dewey
Happiness, Mary Lavin
*Crito**, Plato
*On Liberty**, John Stuart Mill
*Conscience**, Immanuel Kant
A Hunger Artist, Franz Kafka
*Of the Limits of Government**, John Locke
Antigone, Sophocles
*Why Great Revolutions Will Become Rare**, Alexis de Tocqueville
*A Room of One's Own**, Virginia Woolf
In Dreams Begin Responsibilities, Delmore Schwartz

*Selections (Non-fiction selections are taken from longer works.)

APPENDIX C
SELECTED BIBLIOGRAPHY

Aiken, Henry David, "What Is A Liberal Education?" *The New York Review of Books*, Nov. 3, 1966.

Allen, Gay Wilson, *William James* (New York: Viking Press, 1967).

Apel, Willi, "Music Education in the United States," *Harvard Dictionary of Music* (Cambridge: Harvard University Press, 1944).

Aristotle, *The Politics.*

Auden, W. H., "In Memory of W. B. Yeats," "September 1, 1939," *The Collected Poetry of W. H. Auden* (New York: Random House, 1945).

Barzun, Jacques, *Science: The Glorious Entertainment* (New York: Harper and Row, 1964).

Bell, E. T., *Mathematics: Queen and Servant of the Sciences* (New York: McGraw-Hill, 1951).

Bettelheim, Bruno, "Growing Up Female" *Harper's Magazine*, October, 1962.

Blumenfeld, Samuel L., "Why America Has A Reading Problem," *The Education Digest*, October, 1974.

Brann, Eva T. H., *Paradoxes of Education in a Democracy* (Chicago: University of Chicago Press, 1979).

Bruner, Jerome, *The Process of Education* (Cambridge: Harvard University Press, 1960).

Buber, Martin, *Between Man and Man* (New York: The Macmillan Company, 1965); *I and Thou* (2d ed.) Trans. Ronald Gregor Smith (New York: Charles Scribner's Sons, 1958); *The Knowledge of Man* (New York: Harper and Row, 1965).

Buchanan, Scott, *Poetry and Mathematics* (New York: The John C. Day Co., 1929).

Buchner, Soloman, "Why Mathematics Grows," *Journal of the History of Ideas*, Jan-March, 1965.

Cambridge Conference on School Mathematics, *Goals for School Mathematics* (Boston: Houghton Mifflin Co., 1963).

Cameron, Eleanor, "Unforgettable Glimpse," *Wilson Library Bulletin*, October, 1962.

Cary, Joyce, *Art and Reality* (Cambridge, England: Cambridge University Press, 1958).

Copland, Aaron, *Music and Imagination* (Cambridge: Harvard University Press, 1953).

Cottrell, T. L., "The Scientific Textbook as a Work of Art," *Review of English Literature*, October, 1962.

Descartes, Rene, *Discourse on Method*.

Dewey, John, *How We Think* (New York: D.C. Heath & Co., 1933).

Dineson, Isak, *Enrengard* (New York: Random House, 1963).

Dirac, P. A. M., "Evaluation of the Physicist's Picture of Nature," *Scientific American*, May, 1963.

Eastlake, William, "The Biggest Thing Since Custer," *The Atlantic*, September, 1968.

Eddington, A. S., *Space, Time and Gravitation* (Cambridge, England: Cambridge University Press, 1920).

Erskine, John, *The Moral Obligation to be Intelligent* (Indianapolis: Bobbs-Merrill Co., 1915).

Follett, Wilson, *Modern American Usage*, edited and completed by Jacques Barzun (New York: Hill & Wang, 1966).

Fraiberg, Selma, "The American Reading Problem," *Commentary*, June 1965.

Frost, Robert, *The Letters of Robert Frost to Louis Untermeyer* (New York: Holt, Rinehart and Winston, 1963).

Frye, Northrop, "The Developing Imagination," *Learning in Language and Literature* (Cambridge, Mass.: Harvard University Press, 1963).

Gibbon, Edward, *The Autobiography of Edward Gibbon* (New York: Meridian Books, 1961).

Hanslick, Edward, *The Beautiful in Music*, (Indianapolis: The Bobbs-Merrill Co., 1975).

Hardwick, Elizabeth, "Reflections on Fiction," *The New York Review of Books*, February 13, 1969.

Hardy, G. H., "A Mathematician's Apology," *The World of Mathematics*, Vol. IV. (New York: Simon & Schuster, 1956), ed. James R. Newman.

Hempel, Carl G., "On the Nature of Mathematical Truth," *The World of Mathematics*, Vol. III. (New York: Simon & Schuster, 1956), ed. James R. Newman.

Hillson, Maurice, ed. *Elementary Education* (New York: The Free Press, 1967).

Hindemith, Paul, *A Composer's World* (Cambridge: Harvard University Press, 1953).

Holmes, Oliver Wendell, Jr., *The Common Law* (Boston: Little, Brown & Co., 1945).

Hopkins, Gerard Manley, *A Hopkins Reader*, ed. John Pick (Garden City, N.Y.: Doubleday & Co., 1966, Image Books edition).

Hutchins, Robert M., *Some Observations on American Education* (Cambridge: Cambridge University Press, 1956).

Irving, Jerome M., "A Parting Visit with Robert Frost," *Hudson Review,* Spring, 1963.
Joyce, James, *A Portrait of the Artist as a Young Man* (New York: The Viking Press, 1956).

Kant, Immanuel, *Education*, trans. Annette Churton (Ann Arbor, Mich.: University of Michigan Press, 1960).

Karp, Walter, "Why Johnnie Can't Think," *Harper's*, June, 1985.

Kaufmann, Walter, "*I and You*: A Prologue," *I and Thou* by Martin Buber, trans. Walter Kaufman (New York: Charles Scribner's Sons, 1970).

Kemeny, John G., *A Philosopher Looks at Science* (New York: Van Nostrand Co., 1959).

Keyser, Cassius J., *The Human Worth of Rigorous Thinking* (New York: Columbia University Press, 1916).

Kierkegaard, S., *Christian Discourses*, trans. Walter Lowrie (Princeton, N.J.: Princeton University Press, 1971).
    For Self-Examination and Judge for Yourselves Princeton University Press, 1944.
    Either/Or, trans. David F. Swenson and Lillian M. Swenson (Princeton University Press, 1946).

Koerner, James D., *Who Controls American Education?* (Boston, Beacan Press, 1968).

Kusch, Polykarp, "Mathematics in Science Teaching," *The Science Teacher*, May, 1966.

Langer, Suzannne, *Feeling and Form* (New York: Charles Scribner's Sons, 1953).

Le Corbusier and Amadee Ozenfant, "Purism," *Modern Artists in Art*, ed. Robert L. Herbert (Englewood Cliffs, N.J.: Prentice-Hall, Inc., 1964).

Leishman, J.B., "Introduction," Vol.I: *Selected Works*, Rainer Maria Rilke; trans. G. Craig Houston (New York: New Directions, 1961).

Lewis, C. S., "On the Reading of Old Books," *God in the Dock; Essays on Theology and Ethics* (Grand Rapids, Mich.: Wm. B. Eerdmans Publishing Co., 1970).

Locke, John, *On Politics and Education*, ed. Howard R. Penniman (New York: D. Van Nostrand Co., 1947).

MacDonald, John D., *A Purple Place for Dying* (Greenwich, Conn.: Fawcett Publishing Co., 1964).

MacKinnon, Frank, *The Politics of Education* (Toronto: The Unversity of Toronto Press, 1960).

Malraux, Andre, *The Voices of Silence*, trans. Stuart Gilbert (New York: Doubleday & Co., 1953).

Maritain, Jacques, *Education at the Crossroads* (New Haven: Yale University Press, 1943).

Masciantonio, Rudolph, "The New FLES Latin Program in the School District of Philadelphia, "*Modern Language Journal*, 56, 3 (1972).

Mavrogenes, Nancy A., "The Effect of Elementary Latin Instruction on Language Arts Performance," *Elementary School Journal*, 77, 4 (1977).

McKeon, Richard P., "The Liberating Arts and the Humanizing Arts in Education," *Humanistic Education and Western Civilization*, ed. Arthur A. Cohen (New York: Holt, Rinehart and Winston, 1964).

Mendelowitz, Daniel M., *Children Are Artists*, 2d ed. (Stanford, Calif.: Stanford University Press, 1963).

Meyer, Martin, *Where, When and Why: Social Studies in American Schools* (New York: Harper and Row, 1962).

Milton, John, "Of Education" *Complete Prose Works of John Milton* (New Haven: Yale University press, 1959), Vol. II.

Montaigne, Michel, "Of the Education of Children," *Great Books of the Western World* (Chicago: Encylopaedia Britannica, 1952 Vol. 25.

Muir, Edwin, *An Autobiography* (New York: The Seabury Press, 1968).

Muller, Herbert J., *Freedom in the Modern World* (New York: Harper & Bros., 1966).
Neill, A. S., *Summerhill: A Radical Approach to Child Rearing* (New York: Hart Publishing Co., 1960).

Newman, James R., *The World of Mathematics* (New York: Simon & Schuster, 1956), ed.

Nock, Albert J., *Memoirs of a Superfluous Man* (Chicago: Henry Regnery Co., 1964).

O'Flaherty, James C. *Unity and Language: A Study in the Philosophy of Johann Georg Hamann* (Chapel Hill, N.C.: University of North Carolina Studies in the Germanic Languages and Literature, 1952).

Ortega y Gasset, José, *The Mission of the Librarian* (Boston: G. K. Hall & Co., 1961).

Orwell, George, *The Collected Essays, Journalism and Letters of George Orwell*, ed. Sonia Orwell and Ian Angus (New York: Harcourt, Brace & World, Inc., 1968).

Pascal, Blaise, "On Geometrical Demonstration," *Great Books of the Western World* (Chicago: Encyclopaedia Britannica, 1952), Vol. 23.

Penfield, Wilder, "The Uncommitted Cortex," *The Atlantic*, July, 1964.

Plato, "Phaedrus," "Meno," "Apology," Protegoras," *Great Books of the Western World* (Chicago: Encyclopaedia Britannica, 1952), Vol. 24.

Pope, John XXIII, *Pacem in Terris*.

Rabelais, Francois, "Gargantua and Pantagruel," *Great Books of the Western World* (Chicago: Encyclopaedia Britannica, 1952), Vol. 24.

Read, Herbert, *The Grass Roots of Art* (New York: Wittenborn & Co., 1947).

Review of English Literature, editorial, January, 1964.

Richards, I.A., *How to Read a Page* (Boston: Beacon Press, 1959).

Russell, Bertrand, *Mysticism and Logic* (London: George Allen & Unwin Ltd., 1963).

St. John's College, *Catalog 1981-82* (Annapolis, Md.: Santa Fe, N.M.)

Santayana, George, *The Life of Reason*, 1 vol. ed. (New York: Charles Scribner's Sons, 1953).

Schopenhauer, Arthur, *The World as Will and Idea*, trans. R. B. Haldane and J. Kemp Claudon (London: Routledge and Kegan Paul Ltd., 1983), Vol. 1
  The Art of Literature (Ann Arbor: The University of Michigan Press, 1960).

Schwab, Joseph J., *The Teaching of Science as Inquiry* (Cambridge, Mass: Harvard University Press, 1962).

Shahn, Ben, *The Shape of Content* (Cambridge, Mass.: Harvard University Press, 1957).

Stone, Marshall, "The Revolution in Mathematics," *Liberal Education*, May, 1961.

Ronald Arthur Landor was a school dropout at age fifteen. Fourteen years later under the G.I. bill, he entered the University of California at Berkeley, from which he subsequently received several degrees. He is the father of two sons and four daughters.